CRYPTID DETECTIVES

Case Studies in Modern Cryptozoology Investigations

Mournheart Publishing

CONTENTS

INTRODUCTION TO CRYPTOZOOLOGY

W hat is Cryptozoology?
Cryptozoology, a term that combines "crypto" (meaning hidden or secret) and "zoology" (the study of animals), refers to the investigation of animals whose existence is disputed or unverified by science. These creatures, often referred to as cryptids, exist in the liminal space between folklore and scientific possibility. Famous examples include Bigfoot, the Loch Ness Monster, and the Yeti. While mainstream science often dismisses the existence of these creatures due to a lack of verifiable evidence, cryptozoologists remain dedicated to unraveling these mysteries through field research, eyewitness accounts, and technology.

The field of cryptozoology has its roots in ancient mythologies, where creatures such as mermaids, dragons, and sea serpents dominated the imagination of sailors and adventurers. These creatures were thought to explain unknown phenomena or were seen as supernatural manifestations of human fears. As modern science developed, many of these mythical creatures were debunked, but some continued to capture the public's fascination, becoming more deeply entrenched in popular culture.

Cryptozoology is unique in that it blurs the lines between

scientific inquiry and storytelling. Although cryptozoologists use investigative methods similar to those employed by traditional zoologists—such as tracking, field observation, and biological sampling—their subjects remain elusive, existing primarily in anecdotal evidence, folklore, and cultural memory.

The Origins of Cryptozoology as a Field

While the term cryptozoology was first coined in the mid-20th century, the pursuit of mysterious creatures has been part of human history for millennia. Many ancient civilizations spoke of strange, elusive beasts inhabiting the wilderness, some of which we now know were based on real animals. For example, ancient Greek myths about the one-eyed Cyclops are believed to have originated from the discovery of prehistoric elephant skulls, which have a large central nasal cavity that could be mistaken for a single eye socket.

It wasn't until the 1950s that cryptozoology began to emerge as a more formal field of study, thanks to pioneers like Bernard Heuvelmans, a Belgian-French zoologist often credited as the "father of cryptozoology." In his seminal book, *On the Track of Unknown Animals* (1955), Heuvelmans argued that the search for hidden or unknown animals was a legitimate scientific pursuit. He suggested that many "cryptids" might be surviving members of species thought to be extinct or undiscovered species altogether. Heuvelmans's work inspired a new generation of researchers who sought to bridge the gap between science and myth.

Around the same time, other investigators began taking cryptozoology more seriously. Ivan T. Sanderson, a British biologist and author, was another major figure in the field. He explored phenomena such as Bigfoot, the Yeti, and other cryptids, often combining scientific analysis with cultural exploration.

Defining Cryptids

What exactly qualifies as a cryptid? The definition can be surprisingly fluid, but generally, cryptids are animals or creatures whose existence has been suggested but not proven. This can include creatures that are entirely unknown to science or animals believed to be extinct but persist in folklore or anecdotal sightings.

Some cryptids are well-known creatures of legend, such as Bigfoot, Nessie (the Loch Ness Monster), or the Chupacabra. Others are less familiar but just as mysterious, like Orang Pendek (a supposed bipedal primate in Indonesia) or Mokele-Mbembe, an alleged dinosaur-like creature in the Congo River Basin.

The diversity of cryptids is remarkable, ranging from sea monsters and lake-dwelling serpents to hairy hominids, giant birds, and even extraterrestrial beings. These creatures often become symbols of regional folklore and mythology, embodying local fears, hopes, or mysteries. For example, the Jersey Devil has become an icon in New Jersey, USA, while the Yowie holds a similar status in Australia.

Cryptozoology: Science or Pseudoscience?

One of the primary challenges cryptozoologists face is the question of legitimacy. Many in the scientific community dismiss cryptozoology as pseudoscience due to its reliance on anecdotal evidence, the lack of verifiable physical proof, and its association with the supernatural. However, cryptozoologists argue that their field is a continuation of the scientific quest to discover new species and understand the world's biodiversity.

The discovery of animals like the Okapi (a forest-dwelling mammal in Africa, related to giraffes) and the Coelacanth (a prehistoric fish thought to be extinct but rediscovered in 1938) serves as encouragement to cryptozoologists. Both creatures were once considered myths until scientists found concrete evidence of their existence. These discoveries remind us that the natural world still holds many secrets and that some cryptids might one day be proven to exist.

Skeptical Criticism and Rational Explanations
The most common criticism of cryptozoology is its frequent reliance on eyewitness testimony, which can be unreliable. Human perception is easily influenced by environmental factors, psychological conditions, and cultural narratives. Many "cryptid sightings" can often be explained by misidentifications of known animals or phenomena. For example, many reported lake monsters could be logs or large fish seen in low light, and numerous Bigfoot sightings have turned out to be bears.

While these natural explanations satisfy most skeptics, cryptozoologists remain undeterred. They argue that dismissing cryptid sightings outright could lead to missed opportunities for discovery. Instead, they advocate for a balanced approach —one that combines healthy skepticism with a willingness to investigate.

The Intersection of Folklore and Science
Cryptids often emerge from the intersection of folklore and science. They embody deep-seated cultural narratives, often reflecting the fears or mysteries of their respective societies. For instance, the Mothman, first sighted in West Virginia in the 1960s, is sometimes seen as an omen of disaster. Many cryptids are tied to specific regions and become part of the local identity.

Folklore provides a fertile ground for cryptozoologists, who analyze traditional tales to identify patterns and potential connections to real-world animals or events. Some cryptozoologists hypothesize that ancient encounters with cryptids could explain the origins of some myths. For example, the idea of giant, dragon-like creatures might be rooted in ancient humans' discoveries of dinosaur bones, leading to the belief in dragons.

At the same time, folklore can complicate cryptozoological investigations. Stories and legends often exaggerate or distort the truth, making it difficult to separate fact from fiction. This tension is at the heart of cryptozoology: How do you discern whether a creature exists when the available evidence is primarily anecdotal?

BIGFOOT: THE ELUSIVE GIANT OF THE FOREST

Introduction to the Bigfoot Phenomenon
Bigfoot, also known as Sasquatch, is among the most well-known cryptids in the world, and its legend has been entrenched in North American folklore for centuries. The iconic image of a massive, bipedal, ape-like creature trudging through dense forests has captivated the imaginations of cryptozoologists, nature lovers, and adventurers alike. Sightings are frequently reported across the Pacific Northwest, but stories of Bigfoot-like creatures stretch from Alaska to Florida, under different regional names such as Skunk Ape or Grassman.

The mystery surrounding Bigfoot has evolved into more than a legend; it has become a cultural phenomenon, blending together indigenous myths, eyewitness accounts, hoaxes, and scientific investigations. This chapter dives deep into the origins of the Bigfoot legend, the landmark cases that shaped its narrative, and the methods cryptozoologists use to hunt for evidence of the elusive creature. From footprint casts to the famed Patterson-Gimlin film, we will also explore the challenges and ongoing debates that plague the hunt for definitive proof of Bigfoot's existence.

The Ancient Roots of Sasquatch in Native American Lore

Long before the term "Bigfoot" became popularized in the 20th century, indigenous tribes across North America shared stories of giant, hairy wild men who roamed the forests and mountains. To many Native American cultures, these beings were not mythical but rather considered a natural part of the wilderness, existing somewhere between humans and animals. The Coast Salish people of the Pacific Northwest referred to them as Sasquatch, meaning "wild man" or "hairy man," a term that directly influenced the modern name for Bigfoot.

The Sts'ailes First Nation have passed down oral histories of Sasq'ets, a guardian of the forest, who is described as a large, hairy humanoid. Sasq'ets was believed to live deep in the woods, avoiding human contact, but occasionally being seen by those who ventured too far into its territory. These stories, which have been told for centuries, often reflect reverence for the power and mystery of nature, with Sasq'ets embodying both the fear and respect humans have for the untamed wilderness.

The concept of wild men is not exclusive to North American indigenous cultures. Many societies around the world, including those in Asia and Europe, have similar stories of mysterious forest dwellers. For example, the Yeti of the Himalayas and the Almas of Mongolia bear striking similarities to the Sasquatch legends. These creatures, often referred to as reclusive, intelligent, and physically imposing, are central to the folklore of remote and wooded areas, which suggests a deep-rooted human need to explain the unknown through the lens of creatures that bridge the gap between humans and the wild.

The Rise of Bigfoot in Modern Times

While Native American lore laid the groundwork, Bigfoot did not capture the full public imagination until the mid-20th century. The modern Bigfoot phenomenon truly began in 1958, when construction worker Jerry Crew found large, human-like footprints near Bluff Creek, Northern California. Measuring over 16 inches long, the prints were far larger than any known human or animal could leave. Crew took plaster casts of the prints, and when the story was reported in the press, it coined the now-famous term "Bigfoot."

While skepticism surrounded the discovery, the Bluff Creek incident ignited widespread interest. Bluff Creek would later become the epicenter of the Bigfoot craze, thanks to another pivotal event: the Patterson-Gimlin film, shot in the same region nine years later.

The Patterson-Gimlin Film: A Cryptozoological Icon

The Patterson-Gimlin film, shot in 1967, is perhaps the most famous and controversial piece of evidence in Bigfoot lore. The grainy footage shows what appears to be a large, bipedal creature—later dubbed Patty—walking through a clearing before disappearing into the forest. Filmmakers Roger Patterson and Bob Gimlin were on horseback in Bluff Creek, California, searching for evidence of Bigfoot when they encountered the creature. They managed to capture roughly 60 seconds of footage that has been studied, debated, and dissected by both believers and skeptics for decades.

The debate over the authenticity of the film remains fierce. Supporters argue that the film shows a creature with distinct muscle movement, natural gait, and proportions that would be difficult to fake with the costume technology available in the 1960s. Skeptics, on the other hand, claim that the film depicts a man in a suit, citing the convenience of the encounter, the poor quality of the footage, and the lack of subsequent, equally compelling evidence.

However, the Patterson-Gimlin film has become more than just a piece of evidence; it is a cultural touchstone. For many cryptozoologists, it remains one of the best pieces of visual evidence ever captured of a cryptid. Even for skeptics, the film has become a symbol of the enduring mystery of Bigfoot.

Notable Sightings and Encounters Across the United States

Beyond Bluff Creek, Bigfoot sightings have been reported across the United States, with concentrations in the Pacific Northwest, the Appalachian region, and parts of the Midwest. These encounters vary from fleeting glimpses to close encounters, often accompanied by footprints, strange sounds, or reports of foul odors—an attribute frequently associated with Bigfoot.

1. Skookum Cast (2000):

During an expedition in Skookum Meadow, Washington, a research team discovered what they believed to be a Bigfoot body impression in the mud. Known as the Skookum Cast, the impression included details of a large foot, leg, and buttocks, as if a large creature had sat down in the soft earth. While some skeptics argue the impression was left by an elk, others believe it could be the most significant physical evidence of Bigfoot to date.

2. The Paul Freeman Footage (1994):

Paul Freeman, a U.S. Forest Service worker and avid Bigfoot researcher, captured video footage of a large, bipedal creature in the Blue Mountains of Washington. The footage, while grainy, has been analyzed extensively, with some experts believing the creature's size and gait suggest it is a genuine Bigfoot sighting.

3. The Marble Mountain Encounter (2001):

In Northern California, a youth group leader filmed what he believed was a Bigfoot standing on a ridge, silhouetted against the sky. The footage shows a tall, upright figure with long arms and a sloping back. While the distance makes it difficult to determine details, the Marble Mountain footage has become another significant piece of Bigfoot lore.

Investigative Techniques: Hunting for Bigfoot

Over the decades, cryptozoologists and enthusiasts have developed numerous techniques to try to prove Bigfoot's existence. From casting footprints to collecting hair samples, each method comes with its own set of challenges and controversies.

1. Footprint Analysis and Casting:

One of the most common forms of Bigfoot evidence is the discovery of footprints. These are typically large—between 15 and 24 inches in length—and show a bipedal gait. Investigators create plaster casts of the prints to analyze their depth, stride, and anatomical features, such as toes and arches. While many footprint discoveries have been debunked as hoaxes, some, like the Bluff Creek prints, continue to fuel the mystery.

Footprint analysis is often the first step in a Bigfoot investigation, but it is not without complications. The prints are subject to erosion and distortion, making it difficult to draw definitive conclusions. Additionally, hoaxers have been known to create false prints using carved wooden feet or molds, further complicating efforts to gather reliable evidence.

2. Audio Recordings and Vocalizations:

Many Bigfoot sightings are accompanied by reports of strange vocalizations. These include howls, screams, growls, and wood-knocking sounds (thought to be a form of communication). Audio recordings of these sounds are often analyzed by cryptozoologists to determine whether they could be made by known animals or if they indicate an unknown species.

For example, the Sierra Sounds recordings, captured in the Sierra Nevada mountains in the 1970s, are some of the most famous Bigfoot vocalizations. The recordings feature a series of howls and guttural noises that have been analyzed by audio experts. While some argue the sounds could belong to an unidentified primate, skeptics suggest they may be misidentified animal calls or outright fabrications.

3. Hair and DNA Evidence:
One of the most exciting possibilities for proving Bigfoot's existence lies in DNA analysis. Researchers occasionally find tufts of hair, scat, or other biological material believed to belong to the creature. These samples are sent to laboratories for analysis, but the results are often inconclusive. Many hair samples are identified as belonging to known animals, such as bears or deer. However, some tests have produced unknown or unclassified DNA, which cryptozoologists point to as possible evidence of an unidentified species.

A notable example is the work of Dr. Melba Ketchum, a veterinarian who led a controversial study in 2013 that claimed to have sequenced Bigfoot DNA. Ketchum's study suggested that Bigfoot was a hybrid species—part human, part unknown primate. However, the study was met with skepticism, and mainstream scientists dismissed the findings due to questionable methodology.

Challenges in Proving Bigfoot's Existence
Proving Bigfoot's existence remains an elusive goal for cryptozoologists. Despite decades of research, expeditions, and sightings, no definitive physical evidence—such as a body or clear DNA—has been found. This absence of conclusive proof fuels skepticism and hinders the field of cryptozoology from gaining broader scientific credibility.

Several challenges contribute to the difficulty of proving Bigfoot's existence:

The Vast Wilderness: Many Bigfoot sightings occur in remote, forested areas where the environment is dense and difficult to navigate. This makes it challenging to track the creature, especially if it is adept at avoiding humans.

Lack of Physical Remains: One of the most significant obstacles is the lack of a body or bones. Skeptics argue that if a population of large primates existed in North America, we would have found remains by now. Bigfoot researchers counter that the wilderness is vast and that natural decomposition and scavengers could quickly eliminate any trace of a dead animal.

Hoaxes and Misidentifications: The Bigfoot phenomenon has been plagued by hoaxes and misidentifications, which undermine legitimate research efforts. From fabricated footprints to staged photos and videos, hoaxes have created an atmosphere of skepticism around Bigfoot investigations.

Case Study: The 1967 Patterson-Gimlin Film
The Patterson-Gimlin film continues to be one of the most iconic and debated pieces of Bigfoot evidence. The film has been analyzed by countless experts, from anthropologists to film technicians, yet no consensus has been reached on its authenticity. Several aspects of the film have been scrutinized:

Muscle Movement: Supporters of the film point to the visible muscle movement in the creature's arms and legs, which they argue would be difficult to replicate with a costume in the 1960s.

Proportions: The creature in the film appears to have a longer arm-to-leg ratio than a human, a feature that has led some experts to conclude that it is not a man in a suit.

Gait Analysis: The creature's walk has been studied extensively. The fluidity of its movement, particularly the way it shifts its weight and swings its arms, is considered by some to be inconsistent with a person wearing a bulky costume.

However, skeptics point out several red flags:

Timing and Motivation: Roger Patterson was an amateur filmmaker with a strong interest in Bigfoot. Critics suggest that he may have staged the sighting to promote his work and capitalize on the growing Bigfoot craze.

Costume Technology: Some costume experts argue that it would have been possible to create a convincing suit with the materials available at the time, particularly if the film quality was grainy and the encounter brief.

The truth behind the Patterson-Gimlin film may never be known, but its impact on Bigfoot research and popular culture is undeniable. It remains a symbol of the enduring mystery of Bigfoot, inspiring generations of researchers to continue the search.

Modern Expeditions and the Quest for Proof

Despite the setbacks, Bigfoot research continues in the 21st century, driven by a new generation of cryptozoologists armed with advanced technology. Today's researchers use a combination of traditional tracking methods and cutting-edge tools to increase their chances of capturing evidence.

1. Thermal Imaging and Night Vision:

Many Bigfoot researchers believe the creature is nocturnal, which has led to the widespread use of thermal imaging and night vision cameras during field expeditions. These tools allow researchers to detect heat signatures and movement in low-light conditions, providing a potential edge in the search for an elusive, nocturnal creature.

2. Drone Technology:

Drones equipped with high-resolution cameras and thermal sensors are increasingly being used in Bigfoot investigations. Drones can cover large areas of difficult terrain and provide aerial views of regions where it would be nearly impossible to search on foot. While no definitive Bigfoot sightings have been made with drones, the technology holds promise for future expeditions.

3. Citizen Science and Public Involvement:

The rise of the internet and social media has allowed for the growth of citizen science in cryptozoology. Organizations like the Bigfoot Field Researchers Organization (BFRO) encourage people to report sightings, upload photos and videos, and participate in local investigations. This grassroots approach has led to a surge in reported sightings and has helped bring the Bigfoot phenomenon into the mainstream.

Conclusion: The Enduring Mystery of Bigfoot

The search for Bigfoot represents the larger human desire to explore the unknown and challenge the boundaries of scientific knowledge. Despite decades of research, sightings, and speculation, the creature remains elusive, with no conclusive evidence to prove its existence. Yet, Bigfoot continues to captivate imaginations and inspire new generations of cryptozoologists.

Whether Bigfoot is a surviving species of Gigantopithecus, a relic of prehistoric North America, or a product of collective folklore and misidentification, its legend endures as one of the most fascinating mysteries in cryptozoology.

THE LOCH NESS MONSTER: SCOTLAND'S AQUATIC ENIGMA

Introduction to the Loch Ness Monster
The Loch Ness Monster, affectionately known as Nessie, has captured the world's imagination as one of the most famous aquatic cryptids in history. For centuries, tales of a mysterious creature inhabiting the depths of Loch Ness, a large freshwater loch in the Scottish Highlands, have persisted, with modern sightings continuing to fuel the legend.

Nessie's story transcends the boundaries of local folklore, becoming a global phenomenon in cryptozoology. Descriptions of the creature often resemble a plesiosaur, a long-extinct marine reptile from the Mesozoic Era, leading some to believe that the loch could harbor a living fossil.

This chapter delves into the origins of the Loch Ness Monster, the scientific expeditions and technological advancements used to search for the creature, and the enduring appeal of Nessie in popular culture. We will examine historical sightings, explore the role of hoaxes, and investigate modern theories surrounding the creature's existence.

The Origins of the Loch Ness Monster Legend

The legend of the Loch Ness Monster has its roots in ancient Scottish folklore. Stories of water horses and kelpies—supernatural creatures believed to inhabit Scotland's lakes and rivers—date back centuries. These water beings were often described as shape-shifters capable of luring humans into the water, where they would meet a watery end.

One of the earliest accounts of a monster in Loch Ness comes from the 6th century, when Saint Columba, an Irish monk, was said to have encountered a "water beast" in the river Ness, which flows from Loch Ness to the North Sea. According to legend, the beast attacked a man swimming in the river, but Saint Columba made the sign of the cross and commanded the creature to retreat, sparing the swimmer's life.

Though the story of Saint Columba is steeped in religious lore, it laid the groundwork for future reports of a creature inhabiting the loch. For centuries, sightings remained sporadic, and the Loch Ness Monster remained a local legend. However, the monster gained international fame in the 20th century, thanks to a series of high-profile sightings and photographs.

The 1933 Spicer Sighting: The Birth of the Modern Legend

The modern era of Loch Ness Monster sightings began in 1933, when George Spicer and his wife claimed to have seen a large, long-necked creature crossing the road near Loch Ness. They described the creature as having a huge, undulating body and a long neck, leading some to speculate that the monster could be a surviving dinosaur, possibly a plesiosaur.

The Spicer sighting was widely reported in the press, sparking renewed interest in Loch Ness and its mysterious inhabitant. Later that year, a motorcyclist named Arthur Grant reported nearly hitting a creature with a long neck and flippers while driving near the loch at night. Grant's description further fueled speculation that the creature was an ancient marine reptile that had somehow survived into the modern era.

These sightings, coupled with others in the following years, helped establish Nessie as a global phenomenon. Tourists flocked to the loch in hopes of catching a glimpse of the creature, and the press eagerly reported each new sighting.

The Surgeon's Photograph: A Hoax for the Ages

In 1934, the Loch Ness Monster gained worldwide attention when The Daily Mail published a photograph that purported to show the creature's long neck and head emerging from the water. The photograph, taken by Robert Kenneth Wilson, a London gynecologist, became known as the Surgeon's Photograph and was widely regarded as definitive proof of the monster's existence.

For decades, the Surgeon's Photograph was considered the most compelling evidence of the Loch Ness Monster. However, in 1994, it was revealed to be a hoax. Christian Spurling, a former big-game hunter, confessed on his deathbed that the photograph was staged using a toy submarine fitted with a model of the creature's head and neck. Spurling had orchestrated the hoax with his stepfather, Marmaduke Wetherell, who had been humiliated years earlier when a Loch Ness Monster investigation he led was debunked as a hoax involving hippopotamus footprints.

Despite the revelation, the Surgeon's Photograph remains one of the most iconic images associated with Nessie and continues to be used in media representations of the monster.

Historical Sightings and the Evolution of Nessie's Image

While the Surgeon's Photograph was a turning point in the Loch Ness Monster's popularity, sightings of Nessie date back centuries, with descriptions evolving over time.

1. Saint Columba's Encounter (565 A.D.):
As mentioned earlier, the earliest known report of a monster in Loch Ness comes from the story of Saint Columba. While this account is religious in nature, it established the idea of a dangerous, otherworldly creature living in the loch.

2. The 1880 Dinsdale Sighting:
One of the first recorded modern sightings occurred in 1880, when D. Mackenzie reported seeing an object resembling a log or upturned boat moving through the water, causing a disturbance. This sighting is notable because it predates the 20th-century Nessie sightings and suggests that the legend may have deeper historical roots.

3. Hugh Gray's Photograph (1933):
In 1933, shortly after the Spicer sighting, Hugh Gray took the first known photograph of the Loch Ness Monster. The blurry image shows a long, serpent-like object in the water, though some skeptics believe it could be a distorted image of a dog retrieving a stick.

Over time, Nessie's image has become synonymous with that of a plesiosaur, thanks to descriptions of a long neck and flippers. While this idea has captivated the public imagination, some researchers argue that the creature could be a giant eel or fish, given the size and depth of the loch.

Scientific Expeditions and the Search for Nessie
The search for the Loch Ness Monster has inspired numerous scientific expeditions, many of which have used advanced technology to scour the loch's murky waters. While no definitive evidence has been found, these expeditions have yielded intriguing data.

1. The Loch Ness Investigation Bureau (1962-1972):

In 1962, a group of British researchers formed the Loch Ness Investigation Bureau (LNIB), an organization dedicated to investigating sightings of the Loch Ness Monster. The LNIB conducted surveillance and took photographs of the loch for over a decade, but no conclusive evidence was found.

2. Operation Deepscan (1987):

One of the largest and most famous Nessie expeditions was Operation Deepscan, which took place in 1987. Using a fleet of boats equipped with sonar, researchers scanned the depths of the loch for signs of a large, underwater creature. The sonar detected several large, moving objects, but further analysis suggested they were most likely schools of fish or debris stirred up from the bottom of the loch.

3. The 2018 DNA Survey:

In 2018, researchers conducted a DNA survey of Loch Ness, analyzing water samples for traces of genetic material. The study found no evidence of a plesiosaur or other large aquatic creature, but it did detect significant amounts of eel DNA, leading some scientists to propose that Nessie could be a giant eel rather than a prehistoric reptile.

Hoaxes, Misidentifications, and Skepticism

The search for the Loch Ness Monster has been complicated by numerous hoaxes and misidentifications. The Surgeon's Photograph is the most famous hoax, but others have plagued the investigation for decades. For example, in 1972, a team of researchers claimed to have photographed a flipper-like appendage, but the image was later dismissed as a case of pareidolia—the human tendency to see patterns, such as faces or familiar objects, in random stimuli.

Skeptics argue that many Nessie sightings can be attributed to misidentified animals, such as otters, deer, or large fish.

Additionally, the wake of boats and driftwood have been mistaken for the creature. The loch's unique geography—its long, narrow shape and steep walls—can create unusual wave patterns that contribute to the illusion of a large, moving object.

Despite the lack of concrete evidence, belief in the Loch Ness Monster persists. The monster's image has become a cultural icon, representing the human fascination with the unknown and the enduring mysteries of the natural world.

Case Study: Operation Deepscan (1987)

One of the most ambitious searches for the Loch Ness Monster took place in 1987 with the launch of Operation Deepscan. Organized by Adrian Shine, a researcher who had been studying the loch for years, Operation Deepscan involved a fleet of 24 boats equipped with high-tech sonar devices. The goal was to create a sonar map of the loch and detect any large, moving objects that could be the Loch Ness Monster.

For several days, the boats swept the loch, scanning its depths and transmitting data to a central control center. The operation detected several large, moving targets deep within the loch, sparking excitement among the researchers. However, further analysis revealed that the targets were likely schools of fish or debris disturbed by the boats.

While Operation Deepscan did not uncover definitive proof of Nessie, it marked a turning point in the scientific study of Loch Ness. The expedition demonstrated the use of modern technology in cryptozoology and laid the groundwork for future investigations. Adrian Shine continued his research at Loch Ness, focusing on the ecology of the loch and the possibility that Nessie sightings could be attributed to natural phenomena.

Contemporary Theories: Eel, Plesiosaur, or Pure Myth?

Theories about the Loch Ness Monster's identity have evolved over time, with three main possibilities emerging:

1. The Giant Eel Theory:
The DNA survey conducted in 2018 found significant amounts of eel DNA in the loch's waters, leading some researchers to propose that Nessie could be an oversized eel. Eels are known to inhabit Loch Ness, and some can grow to substantial sizes. While no eels as large as Nessie have been documented, the giant eel theory remains one of the most plausible explanations for some sightings.

2. The Plesiosaur Theory:
The idea that Nessie could be a living plesiosaur has captured the public imagination for decades. The plesiosaur, a marine reptile that lived during the Mesozoic Era, had a long neck, flippers, and a bulky body—traits often attributed to Nessie. However, paleontologists argue that plesiosaurs were marine animals and would not have been able to survive in a freshwater loch for millions of years. Additionally, the plesiosaur theory is undermined by the lack of any fossil evidence of these creatures living beyond the Cretaceous-Paleogene extinction event.

3. The Myth and Misidentification Theory:
Skeptics argue that Nessie is a product of myth, hoaxes, and misidentifications. The loch's geography, combined with its dark, murky waters, creates an ideal environment for optical illusions and strange wave patterns. Additionally, the human brain's tendency to interpret ambiguous stimuli in familiar terms—such as seeing a long-necked creature where there is only driftwood—could explain many sightings.

Despite the skepticism, the Loch Ness Monster remains an enduring mystery. Whether Nessie is a real creature or a figment of the imagination, the legend continues to captivate people worldwide, drawing tourists to the loch and inspiring countless books, films, and documentaries.

Conclusion: The Loch Ness Monster in Popular Culture

The Loch Ness Monster has transcended its status as a local legend to become a global icon. From its humble beginnings in Scottish folklore to its starring role in films, television shows, and documentaries, Nessie has captured the world's imagination. The creature embodies humanity's fascination with the unknown, the possibility that there are still mysteries lurking in the natural world waiting to be discovered.

Despite the lack of definitive evidence, belief in Nessie persists. For many, the Loch Ness Monster represents the thrill of the hunt for the unknown and the idea that not everything in our world has been explained by science. As long as people continue to search the depths of Loch Ness, the legend of Nessie will endure.

THE JERSEY DEVIL: TERROR IN THE PINE BARRENS

Introduction to the Jersey Devil Legend
The Jersey Devil is one of America's oldest and most enduring cryptids. Said to inhabit the Pine Barrens of southern New Jersey, the creature has been described as having a goat-like head, leathery wings, horns, and hooves. With a reputation for shrieking cries and terrorizing local residents, the Jersey Devil has inspired fear and fascination for over two centuries.

Unlike many cryptids, which are often rooted in vague folklore, the Jersey Devil has a distinct origin story: the tale of Mother Leeds and her 13th child, who was supposedly cursed from birth and transformed into the Jersey Devil. This story, combined with numerous sightings and strange occurrences in the Pine Barrens, has kept the legend alive in American folklore.

This chapter explores the origins of the Jersey Devil, the historical context of the 1909 Panic, and the modern efforts to investigate and debunk the creature. We will also examine the creature's place in New Jersey culture and its continued influence on cryptozoology.

The Legend of Mother Leeds and the Jersey Devil

The most famous origin story of the Jersey Devil begins in 1735 with a woman named Deborah Leeds, also known as Mother Leeds, who lived in the Pine Barrens. According to legend, Mother Leeds, who already had 12 children, cursed her 13th child in a fit of frustration, saying, "Let it be the Devil!" When the baby was born, it transformed into a horrific creature with wings, hooves, and a tail. The creature then flew out of the Leeds' chimney and disappeared into the surrounding wilderness, where it has reportedly haunted the Pine Barrens ever since.

The Leeds family was real, and historical records show that Daniel Leeds, the patriarch, was a controversial figure in colonial New Jersey. Leeds was a Quaker who became embroiled in religious and political disputes, eventually earning a reputation as a supporter of the British monarchy. Some historians suggest that the Jersey Devil legend may have been a form of political propaganda, with Leeds' enemies spreading rumors about his family to discredit him.

Despite the historical context, the legend of the Jersey Devil has taken on a life of its own, with numerous variations and embellishments. Some versions of the story describe the creature as a harbinger of death or disaster, while others portray it as a mischievous trickster. Regardless of the details, the core elements of the Jersey Devil legend—a cursed birth, a monstrous transformation, and a creature haunting the Pine Barrens—remain central to its enduring appeal.

The 1909 Jersey Devil Panic: Mass Hysteria or Genuine Threat?

In January 1909, the legend of the Jersey Devil reached a fever pitch when a series of sightings and strange events sparked a mass panic across southern New Jersey and Philadelphia. Over the course of a week, hundreds of people reported seeing the creature, describing it as a winged, hoofed beast with a blood-curdling scream.

Newspapers of the time reported on the "phantom" with sensational headlines, claiming that the creature had been seen by police officers, firemen, and other reliable witnesses. Some reports even suggested that the Jersey Devil had attacked trolley cars and left strange, hoof-like tracks in the snow.

The panic spread quickly, with schools and factories closing in fear of the creature. Posse groups were formed to hunt the Jersey Devil, and the Philadelphia Zoo even offered a reward for its capture, prompting several hoaxes. One of the most famous hoaxes involved the display of a kangaroo with artificial wings at a local circus.

Historians believe the 1909 panic was likely a case of mass hysteria, fueled by media sensationalism and public fear. However, some cryptozoologists argue that the sheer number of sightings and the consistency of the descriptions suggest that there may have been a real, unknown creature at the heart of the panic.

Investigative Techniques: Hunting for the Jersey Devil

Despite the Jersey Devil's reputation as a creature of folklore, modern cryptozoologists have attempted to investigate sightings and gather evidence of the creature's existence. Some of the techniques used in these investigations include:

1. Eyewitness Testimonies and Interviews:

Much like Bigfoot investigations, many Jersey Devil cases rely on eyewitness accounts. Researchers often interview witnesses to gather detailed descriptions of the creature's appearance and behavior. Consistent elements—such as the goat-like head, bat-like wings, and shrill cry—lend credibility to some sightings, though skeptics argue that these descriptions could be influenced by popular depictions of the creature.

2. Analyzing Tracks and Physical Evidence:

Several reported Jersey Devil sightings have been accompanied by the discovery of hoof-like tracks. Investigators analyze these tracks for patterns and depth, but most have been dismissed as misidentified animal tracks or fabrications. Nevertheless, the discovery of strange footprints in the snow during the 1909 panic remains one of the most intriguing pieces of physical evidence.

3. Audio Recordings:

In recent years, some investigators have focused on recording the strange screeches and cries attributed to the Jersey Devil. These recordings are analyzed to determine if they could be the calls of known animals, such as owls or foxes, both of which are common in the Pine Barrens and are known for their eerie vocalizations.

4. Historical Research:

Some cryptozoologists and historians believe that the Jersey Devil legend may be rooted in misidentifications of natural phenomena or animals. For example, large birds such as the great horned owl or sandhill crane could be mistaken for a winged creature, especially in low light conditions. Others suggest that the legend could have been influenced by the political and religious tensions of the 18th century, particularly the Leeds family's association with British loyalism.

Case Study: The 1909 New Jersey Panic

The **1909 Jersey Devil Panic** is one of the most significant events in the creature's history, marking a turning point in the public's perception of the legend. Over the course of a week in January, dozens of sightings were reported across New Jersey and parts of Pennsylvania, with some witnesses claiming to have seen the creature flying overhead, while others reported hearing its blood-chilling cries.

One of the most dramatic incidents occurred in the town of Woodbury, New Jersey, where police officers claimed to have seen the Jersey Devil flying over the streets. In Bristol, Pennsylvania, a local fireman reported encountering the creature while it was perched on the roof of a building. Another witness claimed that the creature attacked a trolley car in Haddon Heights, New Jersey, leaving claw marks and frightening the passengers.

The discovery of hoof-like tracks in the snow further fueled the panic. The tracks appeared in towns across New Jersey, often leading to bizarre locations, such as the tops of buildings or the edges of frozen lakes. This phenomenon led some to believe that the creature was capable of teleportation or could fly.

As the panic spread, local authorities organized posse groups to hunt the creature. Armed with guns and torches, these groups searched the Pine Barrens and surrounding areas, but no physical evidence was found. The Philadelphia Zoo offered a reward for the capture of the creature, and several hoaxes emerged, including the infamous display of a winged kangaroo at a local circus.

Historians have analyzed the 1909 panic as a classic case of mass hysteria, where fear and rumors spiraled out of control, fueled by sensational media reports. However, cryptozoologists argue that the number of sightings, combined with the consistency of the descriptions, suggests that there may have been a real, unknown creature at the heart of the panic.

Skepticism and Debunking the Jersey Devil
While the legend of the Jersey Devil is deeply ingrained in American folklore, skeptics argue that the creature is nothing more than a myth fueled by misidentifications, hoaxes, and fear of the unknown. Many sightings of the Jersey Devil can be explained by natural phenomena or the presence of large birds or nocturnal animals.

One of the most common explanations for Jersey Devil sightings is the great horned owl, a large bird with horn-like ear tufts and a piercing scream. These owls are common in the Pine Barrens and are known for their eerie calls, which could easily be mistaken for the Jersey Devil's shrieks.

Another potential explanation is the sandhill crane, a tall, long-legged bird with a distinctive call. Sandhill cranes are known to migrate through New Jersey, and their size and shape could be mistaken for a winged creature in flight, especially in low light conditions.

Skeptics also point to the role of pareidolia—the tendency of the human brain to perceive familiar patterns, such as faces or shapes, in random stimuli. In the dense, shadowy forests of the Pine Barrens, it's easy to see how pareidolia could lead to sightings of a creature that isn't really there.

Despite these explanations, belief in the Jersey Devil remains strong, particularly in New Jersey, where the creature has become a cultural icon.

The Jersey Devil in Popular Culture

The Jersey Devil has transcended its status as a regional legend to become a prominent figure in American popular culture. The creature has appeared in books, films, television shows, and even video games, cementing its place in the pantheon of American cryptids.

1. The Jersey Devil in Film and Television:

The Jersey Devil has been the subject of several films, most notably the 1998 horror movie "The Jersey Devil," which portrays the creature as a malevolent force terrorizing a group of campers. The legend has also been featured in popular television shows such as The X-Files, where the creature is depicted as a feral, human-like monster.

2. The Jersey Devil in Sports:

The Jersey Devil's influence extends beyond the realm of

cryptozoology. The New Jersey Devils, a professional hockey team in the National Hockey League (NHL), adopted the creature as their mascot, further solidifying the legend's place in New Jersey culture.

3. The Jersey Devil in Video Games:
The Jersey Devil has also appeared in several video games, including the 1997 PlayStation game "Jersey Devil," in which players control a cartoonish version of the creature as it battles enemies in the Pine Barrens.

Conclusion: The Enduring Legacy of the Jersey Devil
The legend of the Jersey Devil has endured for over two centuries, evolving from a regional folktale into a symbol of New Jersey's rich folklore. Whether real or imagined, the Jersey Devil represents the human desire to explain the unexplainable and the fear of what lurks in the unknown corners of the world.

While skeptics dismiss the Jersey Devil as a myth, the creature continues to capture the imaginations of those who venture into the Pine Barrens in search of the supernatural. The Jersey Devil's place in American cryptozoology is secure, and its legacy will likely continue for generations to come.

CHUPACABRA: THE BLOOD-SUCKING PREDATOR OF THE AMERICAS

I ntroduction to the Chupacabra Phenomenon
The Chupacabra is one of the most infamous and mysterious cryptids of the late 20th century. First reported in Puerto Rico in the mid-1990s, the creature is described as a vampiric predator that preys on livestock, particularly goats, leaving behind mutilated bodies drained of blood. The term Chupacabra, which translates to "goat-sucker" in Spanish, encapsulates this creature's most chilling characteristic: its supposed penchant for blood.

While initially concentrated in Puerto Rico, sightings of the Chupacabra quickly spread across Latin America, the southwestern United States, and even parts of Europe. Like many cryptids, the descriptions of the Chupacabra vary widely, but the most common portrayal is of a reptilian or alien-like creature with spikes running down its back, glowing red eyes, and a long, forked tongue. Some variations describe it as more canine-like, especially in later reports from the mainland U.S.

In this chapter, we'll explore the origins of the Chupacabra legend, dissect the major case studies that popularized its myth, and delve into the scientific analyses and hoaxes that have both fueled and debunked the legend. The Chupacabra represents a cryptid born in the modern media age, spreading fear and fascination across cultures at an unprecedented speed.

Origins of the Chupacabra Myth in Puerto Rico

The Chupacabra legend began in the small town of Canóvanas, Puerto Rico, in 1995, where locals reported a series of bizarre livestock deaths. The bodies of goats, chickens, and other animals were found mutilated, with precise, circular puncture wounds on their necks and completely drained of blood. These attacks baffled authorities, as no known predator left such clean and peculiar wounds, leading some to speculate that an unknown creature was responsible.

The first person to claim a Chupacabra sighting was a woman named Madelyne Tolentino. She described the creature as a small, reptilian being, standing about 4-5 feet tall, with large eyes, spines running down its back, and a grey-green skin. Tolentino's description, remarkably similar to the Grey Alien archetype popularized by UFO culture, ignited a frenzy in the Puerto Rican press, and soon, more witnesses came forward with similar reports.

Within months, the Chupacabra became a media sensation, with the Puerto Rican government even launching a formal investigation into the livestock attacks. Rumors circulated that the creature was the result of a government experiment gone wrong or even an extraterrestrial being left behind after a UFO sighting. The Chupacabra quickly cemented its place as a modern cryptid with a wide range of outlandish and speculative origins.

Physical Descriptions: Reptilian vs. Canine Chupacabras

As the legend of the Chupacabra spread, two distinct physical descriptions of the creature emerged: the reptilian Chupacabra, primarily reported in Puerto Rico and Latin America, and the canine-like Chupacabra, seen in the United States and later reports from Mexico.

1. The Reptilian Chupacabra:
The original reports from Puerto Rico described a bipedal, reptilian creature, often compared to a small alien or lizard-like being. Witnesses consistently mentioned its spiny back, elongated limbs, and glowing red eyes, adding to its supernatural aura. Some accounts even included bat-like wings, suggesting the creature could fly, which intensified its mysterious and terrifying reputation.

2. The Canine Chupacabra:
By the early 2000s, sightings of a four-legged, canine-like creature began to surface in Texas, Arizona, and other parts of the American Southwest. This version of the Chupacabra was described as hairless, with leathery skin, sharp fangs, and a pronounced, hunched posture. Unlike the reptilian version, the canine Chupacabra walked on all fours and was often mistaken for a coyote or wild dog afflicted with mange. These reports suggested that the creature was not a mythical being but rather a misidentified natural predator suffering from a severe skin condition.

While both versions of the Chupacabra share the common trait of blood-draining, the shift from a bipedal reptilian monster to a quadrupedal canine reflects the evolution of the myth as it crossed cultural and geographic boundaries.

Eyewitness Accounts and Mass Hysteria: Puerto Rico to Texas

The 1995 Puerto Rican sightings sparked a wave of mass hysteria, with thousands of people reporting livestock attacks and Chupacabra sightings across the island. This hysteria quickly spread to Mexico, Chile, and other parts of Latin America, where locals similarly began reporting mysterious livestock deaths. While skeptics argued that the wounds could be the result of feral dogs or bats, the precise nature of the puncture marks and the complete blood drainage stoked fear and fascination.

In Texas, Chupacabra hysteria took on a different form. Ranchers and farmers began reporting sightings of strange, hairless creatures killing livestock, often leaving behind desiccated corpses with similar puncture wounds. One of the most famous incidents occurred in 2004, when a rancher named Elmendorf found a hairless, blue-skinned animal on his property that he claimed was the Chupacabra. The creature was later identified as a coyote suffering from mange, but the legend persisted.

Throughout these encounters, eyewitness accounts were often sensationalized by the media, contributing to the growing Chupacabra mythos. News outlets in both Latin America and the U.S. latched onto the creature's enigmatic nature, leading to a feedback loop where each new sighting seemed to confirm the Chupacabra's existence.

Scientific Explanations: Canine Mange and Forensics
While the Chupacabra has captured the public imagination, scientific investigations into livestock deaths and supposed Chupacabra sightings have largely debunked the myth. Most researchers believe that the canine Chupacabra sightings are simply cases of wild animals, such as coyotes, foxes, or dogs, suffering from sarcoptic mange—a condition caused by mites that leads to hair loss, skin thickening, and a feral appearance.

In the case of the Elmendorf beast, DNA analysis confirmed that the creature was a coyote with severe mange, and subsequent Chupacabra sightings across the American Southwest have often been attributed to similarly afflicted animals. Mange causes these animals to become emaciated and weakened, leading them to attack easy prey like livestock, which explains the reports of unusual attacks.

Forensic analysis of livestock deaths associated with the Chupacabra often reveals that the puncture wounds and blood loss are the result of natural predators, such as dogs or coyotes, rather than a mythical creature. In many cases, animals that have been killed by predators may appear to be drained of blood due to post-mortem blood pooling, giving the illusion of exsanguination.

Despite these logical explanations, belief in the Chupacabra persists, particularly in rural communities where unexplained livestock deaths can have a significant economic impact.

Case Study: The 1995 Puerto Rico Chupacabra Incident

The first major investigation into the Chupacabra occurred in 1995, following the initial sightings in Puerto Rico. After a series of livestock deaths in the small town of Canóvanas, local authorities, led by the town's mayor, Jose "Chemo" Soto, launched a formal investigation into the mysterious creature. Soto, an eccentric figure, took the investigation seriously, organizing hunts for the Chupacabra and calling for public vigilance.

Eyewitness reports flooded in, and dozens of animals were found dead, their bodies drained of blood. While some locals believed the attacks were the work of extraterrestrial beings or government experiments, the investigation yielded no definitive proof of a Chupacabra. Scientists and biologists who examined the animal carcasses suggested that feral dogs or bats could have been responsible for the attacks, but this did little to quell the hysteria.

The Puerto Rico case was notable not only for being the first major Chupacabra sighting but also for highlighting the role of cultural context in shaping cryptid narratives. In a country already steeped in UFO and conspiracy culture, the Chupacabra quickly became a symbol of otherworldly fear, transcending the boundaries of traditional folklore and becoming a reflection of modern anxieties.

Modern Investigations and the Chupacabra's Enduring Mystery

Even with the rise of forensic analysis and scientific debunking, the Chupacabra remains a powerful symbol in Latin American and U.S. culture. Cryptozoologists continue to investigate reports of strange livestock deaths, while paranormal investigators explore modern Chupacabra sightings, hoping to uncover new evidence of the creature's existence. While mainstream science dismisses the Chupacabra as a mythical creature born out of misidentifications and media sensationalism, cryptozoologists argue that not all of the cases can be easily explained.

Some modern Chupacabra researchers focus on the possibility that the reptilian version of the Chupacabra, as originally described in Puerto Rico, might be a distinct phenomenon from the canine-like creatures reported in the U.S. They suggest that the biological evidence collected from U.S. sightings (which often turns out to be misidentified coyotes or dogs with mange) does not fully explain the more bizarre, otherworldly descriptions that emerged during the initial Puerto Rican encounters. These researchers point to the uncanny resemblance between Tolentino's description of the creature and the Grey Alien archetype, linking the Chupacabra to the broader UFO and extraterrestrial phenomenon.

While no physical evidence of a Chupacabra has been found, the mystery persists in the popular consciousness. The creature has become a symbol of modern cryptozoology, illustrating how folklore and media can evolve together to create enduring legends. From its origins in Puerto Rico to its migration across the Americas, the Chupacabra continues to captivate people's imaginations and remains a key focus of cryptid investigations.

The Role of the Media in Shaping the Chupacabra Myth

One of the most fascinating aspects of the Chupacabra

phenomenon is the role that media has played in spreading and shaping the legend. Unlike older cryptids such as Bigfoot or Nessie, which were primarily spread through oral tradition and local folklore, the Chupacabra's rise to prominence coincided with the advent of mass media, particularly in Latin America.

In the early 1990s, news outlets, both in print and on television, latched onto the story of a mysterious creature attacking livestock in Puerto Rico. These stories were often sensationalized, with lurid headlines and graphic images of dead animals, which only fueled the hysteria. Within a few months, the story of the Chupacabra had crossed national boundaries, making headlines in Mexico, Chile, and eventually the United States. The Internet, still in its early stages during the mid-1990s, also played a crucial role in the spread of the Chupacabra myth, as chat rooms and forums dedicated to paranormal activity buzzed with new sightings and theories.

The media's influence is evident in the shift from the original reptilian description of the Chupacabra to the more canine-like version seen in the U.S. As the creature's legend migrated north, its appearance began to change, likely influenced by regional media coverage and local folklore. This transformation underscores the power of the media to shape cryptid narratives, particularly in an age of instantaneous global communication.

Conclusion: The Chupacabra in Modern Cryptozoology

The Chupacabra remains a fascinating example of how cryptids can emerge in modern times and quickly embed themselves into the cultural fabric. Despite numerous scientific debunkings, the creature continues to be a subject of fascination, speculation, and fear. Cryptozoologists continue to receive reports of strange, blood-drained animals across the Americas, and while many of these cases are easily explained by natural predators, the Chupacabra myth persists.

The story of the Chupacabra highlights the complex interplay between folklore, media, and modern culture in shaping cryptid legends. Whether viewed as a product of mass hysteria, a modern-day boogeyman, or an as-yet-undiscovered species, the Chupacabra is a reminder that the world of cryptids is as much about human psychology and cultural narrative as it is about undiscovered creatures.

MOTHMAN: PROPHETIC WINGED BEAST OR GOVERNMENT COVER-UP?

Introduction to the Mothman Phenomenon
The Mothman is one of the most enigmatic and chilling cryptids in American folklore. First sighted in the town of Point Pleasant, West Virginia, in 1966, the Mothman is described as a humanoid figure with large, glowing red eyes and massive wings that allow it to fly at incredible speeds. Its sudden appearance, along with a series of other strange occurrences in the area, culminated in the tragic collapse of the Silver Bridge in 1967, killing 46 people.

Unlike many other cryptids, which are viewed as elusive or even benign, the Mothman has been linked to disaster and tragedy, with some believing that it is a harbinger of doom or even a manifestation of supernatural forces. Over the years, reports of Mothman-like creatures have surfaced around the world, often coinciding with catastrophic events, leading to the creature's reputation as a prophetic figure.

This chapter explores the Mothman legend, from its initial sightings to the theories surrounding its origins. We will delve into the psychological and social dynamics that contributed to the panic in Point Pleasant, examine the investigative efforts to capture evidence of the creature, and consider whether the Mothman might be a case of mass hysteria, misidentification, or something more sinister.

The Point Pleasant Sightings of 1966-67

The first recorded Mothman sighting took place on the night of November 12, 1966, when a group of five men digging a grave near Clendenin, West Virginia, reported seeing a large, winged creature fly over their heads. The creature was described as a man-like figure with wings, prompting immediate fear and confusion.

Just a few days later, on November 15, 1966, two young couples —Roger and Linda Scarberry and Steve and Mary Mallette— were driving near an abandoned World War II munitions facility known as the TNT Area, outside of Point Pleasant. The couples claimed to have encountered a tall, humanoid figure with glowing red eyes and wings folded against its back. According to their report, the creature spread its wings and began to chase their car, flying at speeds exceeding 100 mph. The couples fled to the local police station, where they reported their encounter.

Over the next year, dozens of similar sightings were reported around Point Pleasant. Witnesses described a creature with glowing eyes, massive wings, and a frightening, humanoid appearance. The sightings were often accompanied by strange phenomena, such as radio and television interference, strange noises, and reports of UFOs. Local newspapers dubbed the creature the Mothman, drawing on its bat-like appearance and perhaps inspired by the popular Batman character of the time.

As the sightings continued, fear and paranoia spread through

Point Pleasant, with some residents believing that the Mothman was a supernatural entity or even a visitor from another dimension. Others suggested that the creature was a government experiment gone wrong, possibly linked to the nearby TNT Area, which had once been used to manufacture explosives.

The Collapse of the Silver Bridge: Mothman's Dark Prophecy

The Mothman legend took a tragic turn on December 15, 1967, when the Silver Bridge, which connected Point Pleasant to Gallipolis, Ohio, suddenly collapsed during rush hour traffic. Forty-six people were killed in the disaster, and many locals believed that the Mothman sightings had been an omen foretelling the tragedy.

In the aftermath of the collapse, reports of Mothman sightings in the area ceased, leading to speculation that the creature's appearance had been a warning of the impending disaster. Some cryptozoologists and paranormal researchers point to the Mothman's association with the bridge collapse as evidence that the creature possesses prophetic abilities, while others suggest that the sightings and the tragedy were merely coincidental.

The collapse of the Silver Bridge was later attributed to a structural failure, specifically the failure of a single eye-bar chain in the suspension system. However, the timing of the disaster, coming on the heels of a year filled with strange sightings and unexplained phenomena, cemented the Mothman's reputation as a harbinger of doom.

Theories About Mothman: Prophetic Creature or Mass Hysteria?

Since the original sightings, numerous theories have emerged to explain the Mothman phenomenon. These theories range from natural explanations to more paranormal interpretations.

1. The Sandhill Crane Hypothesis:
One of the most common explanations for the Mothman sightings is that the creature was a misidentified sandhill crane. These large birds, which stand about four feet tall and have a wingspan of over six feet, could easily be mistaken for a humanoid figure in poor lighting. The red patches around the crane's eyes may have contributed to the descriptions of glowing red eyes.

Skeptics argue that the Mothman sightings likely resulted from a combination of misidentifications and mass hysteria, with the crane theory providing a plausible natural explanation for the creature's appearance.

2. UFOs and Paranormal Phenomena:
Another popular theory links the Mothman to extraterrestrial activity. During the same period as the Mothman sightings, residents of Point Pleasant reported seeing strange lights in the sky and experiencing electronic disturbances, leading some to believe that the Mothman was either an alien being or somehow connected to UFOs.

In his book *The Mothman Prophecies*, author John Keel suggests that the Mothman was part of a series of paranormal events, including UFO sightings and encounters with Men in Black. Keel's work contributed to the perception of the Mothman as a supernatural entity, possibly even from another dimension.

3. Psychological Theories and Mass Hysteria:
Some researchers suggest that the Mothman phenomenon can be explained by psychological factors, particularly mass hysteria. The sightings of a strange creature, combined with the unexplained phenomena in the area, may have created a feedback loop where fear and paranoia fed further reports of sightings.
The Silver Bridge disaster may have intensified this hysteria, as locals searched for meaning in the wake of the tragedy. In this view, the Mothman legend is seen as a psychological response to

uncertainty and fear, with the creature serving as a scapegoat for the collective anxiety of the community.

4. Government Cover-Up:
A more fringe theory suggests that the Mothman was the result of a government experiment or a biological weapon gone wrong. Proponents of this theory point to the TNT Area—a former munitions site used during World War II—as a potential source of contamination or radioactive mutation. They argue that the Mothman may have been a mutated creature or even a test subject that escaped from a government facility.

Investigating the Mothman: Eyewitness Testimonies and Field Research
Despite the lack of concrete evidence, cryptozoologists and paranormal investigators have spent decades trying to uncover the truth behind the Mothman sightings. Much of the research focuses on eyewitness testimonies, which provide a consistent description of the creature but lack physical evidence.

1. Eyewitness Testimonies:
The most compelling aspect of the Mothman legend is the sheer number of eyewitness accounts. Over a period of 13 months, dozens of people reported seeing the creature, often describing the same characteristics: glowing red eyes, massive wings, and a humanoid form. These accounts were given by a wide range of individuals, including law enforcement officers, teachers, and factory workers, lending credibility to the reports.

Many of the witnesses described feeling an overwhelming sense of dread when encountering the Mothman, as if the creature exuded a malevolent aura. This has led some researchers to suggest that the Mothman may be a psychic entity capable of instilling fear in its victims.

2. Physical Evidence:

Despite the numerous sightings, no physical evidence of the Mothman has ever been found. No footprints, feathers, or other traces of the creature have been recovered, leading skeptics to argue that the sightings were either fabrications or misidentifications of natural animals.

Cryptozoologists who have investigated the Mothman believe that the creature may possess supernatural abilities, allowing it to appear and disappear at will. This theory, while lacking scientific support, has gained traction among those who view the Mothman as a being from another dimension or an extraterrestrial visitor.

3. The TNT Area:
The TNT Area, located just outside Point Pleasant, has been a focal point for Mothman investigations. This sprawling complex of abandoned bunkers and tunnels, once used to store explosives during World War II, is considered the creature's primary habitat. Some researchers believe that the contaminated environment of the TNT Area could have caused mutations in local wildlife, potentially explaining the Mothman's unusual appearance.
The area has also become a popular destination for paranormal investigators and Mothman enthusiasts, who continue to search for evidence of the creature's presence.

Mothman in Popular Culture: From Folklore to Film
Since the original sightings, the Mothman has become a staple of American folklore, inspiring countless books, films, and documentaries. The creature's enduring appeal lies in its connection to disaster and mystery, making it a compelling subject for both cryptozoology and popular culture.

1. The Mothman Prophecies:
In 1975, author John Keel published *The Mothman Prophecies*, a book that explored the Point Pleasant sightings and connected them to a broader pattern of paranormal events. Keel's book, which delved into UFOs, psychic phenomena, and Men in Black,

helped cement the Mothman's status as a supernatural figure.

In 2002, Keel's book was adapted into a feature film starring Richard Gere, bringing the Mothman legend to a global audience. The film, while fictionalized, drew on real events and further popularized the idea that the Mothman is a harbinger of doom.

2. Mothman Festivals and Tourism:
The town of Point Pleasant has embraced its connection to the Mothman legend, hosting an annual Mothman Festival that draws thousands of visitors from around the world. The festival features lectures, tours, and merchandise, celebrating the town's most famous resident.
Point Pleasant is also home to a Mothman Museum and a 12-foot-tall statue of the creature, complete with glowing red eyes and metallic wings. The Mothman has become a major part of the town's identity, attracting both cryptid enthusiasts and casual tourists.

Conclusion: The Enduring Mystery of the Mothman
The Mothman remains one of the most intriguing and mysterious cryptids in American folklore. Whether viewed as a prophetic creature, a product of mass hysteria, or a misidentified animal, the Mothman continues to captivate the imaginations of those who seek to uncover the truth behind its sightings.

The legend of the Mothman serves as a reminder of the psychological and cultural factors that contribute to cryptid phenomena. In times of fear and uncertainty, communities often turn to supernatural explanations for the unexplainable, creating legends that endure long after the events themselves have faded into history.

THUNDERBIRDS: ANCIENT LEGENDS OR LIVING DINOSAURS?

I ntroduction to the Thunderbird Mythos
Among the various cryptids that have been sighted across North America, Thunderbirds stand out as creatures deeply embedded in both indigenous mythology and modern-day sightings. These giant birds are often described as having enormous wingspans, sometimes measuring up to 20 feet or more, and are said to resemble prehistoric creatures, particularly pterosaurs—flying reptiles from the Mesozoic era. Thunderbirds are a fascinating cryptid because they are believed to have the power to control the weather, summon storms, and bring thunder with the flap of their wings.

While many sightings of Thunderbirds can be traced back to Native American oral traditions, in which the birds are seen as powerful, god-like beings, modern accounts often portray them as elusive and fearsome predators capable of carrying away livestock and, in some cases, even children. Reports of these massive birds span the continental United States, with particularly strong concentrations in the Midwest and Appalachian regions.

This chapter will explore the deep cultural roots of the Thunderbird legend in Native American lore, the most famous modern sightings of these giant birds, and the various investigations carried out by cryptozoologists to determine whether these creatures could be surviving members of a species long thought to be extinct.

Thunderbirds in Native American Folklore

To understand the modern mystery of Thunderbirds, one must first explore their significance in Native American mythology. The Thunderbird is considered a sacred being in many indigenous cultures, especially among tribes in the Pacific Northwest and Great Plains regions. In these traditions, Thunderbirds are often depicted as protectors and bringers of both life and destruction.

For the Lakota Sioux, for example, Thunderbirds are viewed as divine messengers that live in the highest reaches of the sky, controlling thunder and lightning. The birds are believed to have great power, capable of causing devastating storms when they fly and battles between rival Thunderbirds are thought to result in severe weather phenomena such as thunderstorms or tornados. Similarly, for the Algonquian tribes, Thunderbirds were revered as creators of rain and harvests, bringing life to crops and ensuring the survival of their people.

Across Native American cultures, the Thunderbird is portrayed as a massive, majestic bird, often adorned with bright, colorful feathers, sharp talons, and a powerful beak. These features closely resemble the modern description of Thunderbirds seen by witnesses in various parts of the United States.

The symbolic and spiritual importance of Thunderbirds has caused them to endure for centuries, with these legendary beings becoming more than just myth. They embody the natural forces that indigenous peoples respected and feared, serving as metaphors for the unpredictability and raw power of nature.

Modern Sightings: Could Thunderbirds Be Real?

While Thunderbirds have long been a part of Native American folklore, sightings of massive birds that resemble these mythical creatures have continued into modern times. The first notable Thunderbird sighting of the 20th century occurred in April 1948, near Alton, Illinois. Witnesses reported seeing a gigantic bird with an estimated wingspan of over 20 feet flying above them. The creature's size was so immense that it cast a shadow on the ground, and it flew low enough for witnesses to clearly make out its features.

Later that same year, a similar bird was spotted in Overland, Missouri, where residents described it as looking like "a prehistoric bird." The 1948 sightings are considered some of the most credible in Thunderbird lore because they were reported by multiple people, and there were no known large birds in the area that could match the size and description given by witnesses.

In 1977, one of the most famous modern Thunderbird cases occurred in Lawndale, Illinois. Two young boys, Marlon Lowe and his friend, were playing outside when they saw two giant birds circling overhead. According to Lowe, one of the birds swooped down and actually lifted him off the ground before dropping him after a short distance. While skeptics argue that large birds of prey, such as golden eagles or condors, might have been responsible, Lowe insists that the bird was much larger than any known species, with a wingspan far exceeding that of typical birds of prey.

Other sightings of giant birds have been reported throughout the United States, particularly in Pennsylvania, Texas, and Arizona, where witnesses claim to have seen massive flying creatures soaring through the sky. These accounts often describe the birds as having wingspans ranging from 12 to 20 feet, with some witnesses comparing the creatures to pterosaurs or teratorns, an extinct family of giant birds that lived in North and South America.

Cryptozoological Investigations and Theories

In the world of cryptozoology, the theory that Thunderbirds could be living dinosaurs—specifically pterosaurs—has gained traction over the years. Some researchers believe that certain species of pterodactyls or pteranodons, which were believed to have gone extinct during the Cretaceous-Paleogene extinction event, may have survived in remote areas of the world, particularly in the uncharted regions of South America and Africa. These creatures, according to this theory, might occasionally make their way into more populated areas, leading to the sporadic sightings of Thunderbirds.

The idea of surviving pterosaurs is not new in cryptozoology. For decades, researchers have investigated sightings of large, reptilian birds in Papua New Guinea, where the locals speak of the Ropen, a nocturnal flying creature with a long tail and bat-like wings. The Ropen is often compared to the pterosaur, and cryptozoologists like Jonathan Whitcomb have conducted numerous expeditions to find evidence of the creature, though no conclusive proof has yet been uncovered.

Other researchers believe that Thunderbirds may be misidentified teratorns, a family of giant birds that lived during the Pleistocene epoch. The most famous member of this family, the Argentavis magnificens, had a wingspan of up to 23 feet, making it one of the largest birds to have ever flown. While teratorns are believed to have gone extinct around 10,000 years ago, some cryptozoologists argue that small populations could have survived in remote regions, much like other animals thought to be extinct, such as the coelacanth or the Okapi.

Beyond pterosaurs and teratorns, some researchers suggest that Thunderbirds might be undiscovered species of raptors or condors. In areas like the American Southwest, where large birds such as California condors and Andean condors are known to exist, it is possible that certain sightings of Thunderbirds could be exaggerated accounts of these massive scavengers. With wingspans of up to 10 feet, condors are already among the largest birds in the world, and under the right conditions, they could be mistaken for even larger creatures.

Case Study: The 1977 Lawndale, Illinois Incident

The Lawndale, Illinois Thunderbird incident remains one of the most well-documented and compelling cases of a modern Thunderbird sighting. On July 25, 1977, ten-year-old Marlon Lowe was playing outside his family's home with several other children when two large birds appeared overhead. Lowe described the birds as huge, with wingspans of at least 10 feet. One of the birds swooped down and actually grabbed Lowe by his shoulders, lifting him a few feet off the ground before dropping him.

The incident was witnessed by several adults, including Marlon's mother, Ruth Lowe, who corroborated her son's account. According to Ruth, the bird that attacked Marlon was "black, with a white ring around its neck, and a wingspan like I've never seen before." She described the bird's talons as being incredibly large, easily capable of picking up a small child.

In the aftermath of the attack, local authorities and wildlife experts were called in to investigate. The leading theory was that the bird was a large raptor, possibly a golden eagle or turkey vulture. However, the witnesses insisted that the bird was far larger than any known species in the area. Some cryptozoologists speculated that the bird could have been a condor or even a surviving teratorn, though no definitive evidence was found.

The Lawndale incident remains a central piece of Thunderbird lore, with many researchers pointing to it as one of the strongest pieces of evidence that these giant birds may exist. Despite the skepticism of wildlife experts, the Lowe family has stood by their account for over 40 years.

Investigative Techniques: Analyzing Thunderbird Sightings

Investigating reports of Thunderbirds poses several challenges, primarily because the sightings are often fleeting, and the vast regions where these creatures are said to live make it difficult to conduct thorough searches. Cryptozoologists typically rely on a combination of eyewitness testimony, photographs, and track analysis to investigate Thunderbird sightings, but physical evidence is often lacking.

1. Eyewitness Testimony:

As with many cryptids, Thunderbird sightings rely heavily on the credibility of the witnesses. Investigators typically conduct interviews with those who claim to have seen the creature, looking for consistency in the descriptions of its size, color, and behavior. In some cases, multiple witnesses from different locations report seeing similar creatures, adding weight to the sightings. However, eyewitness testimony can be unreliable due to factors such as distance, lighting conditions, and memory distortion over time.

2. Photograph and Video Analysis:

Photographs and videos of alleged Thunderbirds are rare, but some investigators have managed to capture images of large birds that they believe could be Thunderbirds. These images are often analyzed for scale, using landmarks or other objects in the frame to estimate the size of the bird. Unfortunately, many Thunderbird photographs are either too blurry or taken from such a distance that it is difficult to make accurate measurements.

In one of the most famous cases of Thunderbird photography, a photograph purportedly showing a giant bird nailed to a barn circulated widely in the early 20th century. While the image has become part of Thunderbird lore, no known copies of the photograph exist today, and many believe it to be either a hoax or a misidentification of a large condor.

3. Track Analysis:
In some instances, Thunderbird sightings are accompanied by the discovery of large bird tracks. These tracks are analyzed to determine their size, depth, and shape, with researchers looking for features that might distinguish the prints from those of known birds. However, as with many cryptid investigations, the tracks are often found in remote areas where the ground is soft, making it difficult to preserve the prints for detailed analysis.

Skepticism and Debunking the Thunderbird Myth
Despite the numerous sightings of Thunderbirds over the years, skeptics argue that the majority of these reports can be attributed to misidentified large birds, such as eagles, condors, or even pelicans. In particular, the California condor, which once ranged across much of North America before its population dwindled in the 20th century, has been suggested as the most likely candidate for many Thunderbird sightings.

Condors are among the largest flying birds in the world, with wingspans that can exceed 10 feet, and their presence in remote areas could easily lead to exaggerated reports of their size. Additionally, certain species of raptors and vultures are capable of soaring at great heights, making them appear larger than they actually are when viewed from the ground.

Skeptics also point to the lack of physical evidence—such as bones, feathers, or nests—as a major obstacle to proving the existence of Thunderbirds. If these birds are as large as reported, there should be some remnants of their presence, such as carcasses or skeletal remains. The absence of such evidence, along with the fact that most Thunderbird sightings occur in isolated or sparsely populated areas, has led many to dismiss the creature as a product of folklore and imagination.

Conclusion: Thunderbirds as Myth, Mystery, and Cryptid

The legend of the Thunderbird is a powerful reminder of how mythology and modern sightings can intertwine, creating a cryptid that exists at the crossroads of ancient beliefs and contemporary mysteries. Whether the Thunderbird is a living dinosaur, an undiscovered species of bird, or simply a mythological being that persists in the minds of those who see it, the creature holds a special place in the world of cryptozoology.

For Native Americans, the Thunderbird represents the immense power of nature, capable of bringing both destruction and renewal. For cryptozoologists, it represents the possibility that there are still giant creatures soaring through the skies, waiting to be discovered.

Though skeptics may argue that Thunderbirds are nothing more than misidentified birds or relics of folklore, the enduring fascination with these giant, storm-bringing creatures ensures that the legend will continue to capture imaginations for generations to come.

YETI: THE ABOMINABLE SNOWMAN OF THE HIMALAYAS

Introduction to the Yeti Legend

The Yeti, often referred to as the Abominable Snowman, is one of the most famous cryptids in the world, with a legend rooted in the Himalayan Mountains. Described as a large, ape-like creature that roams the snow-covered peaks of Nepal, Tibet, and Bhutan, the Yeti has fascinated explorers, adventurers, and cryptozoologists for centuries.

Unlike other cryptids, which are often dismissed as mere folklore, the Yeti has been the subject of numerous serious expeditions, including investigations by respected scientists and mountaineers. The creature is often compared to Bigfoot, though its habitat and characteristics set it apart. While Bigfoot is typically associated with temperate forests and remote wilderness areas, the Yeti is believed to inhabit the extreme altitudes of the Himalayas, making it one of the most elusive cryptids in the world.

In this chapter, we will explore the origins of the Yeti legend, examine the major expeditions that have attempted to find evidence of the creature, and delve into the scientific investigations and DNA analyses that have sought to explain the mystery of the Abominable Snowman.

The Yeti in Sherpa Tradition

The legend of the Yeti is deeply intertwined with the religious and spiritual beliefs of the Sherpa people, who live in the high-altitude regions of Nepal and Tibet. In Sherpa culture, the Yeti is not seen as a cryptid or a monster, but rather as a guardian of the mountains, a powerful being that exists between the human world and the spirit world.

According to Sherpa lore, the Yeti, also known as the Meh-Teh, is a bipedal creature covered in thick fur, standing between 6 and 10 feet tall. The Yeti is said to be immensely strong and capable of surviving in the harsh, unforgiving climate of the Himalayan peaks. The creature is often described as shy and reclusive, avoiding human contact and living in the most remote and inaccessible areas of the mountains.

In some stories, the Yeti is a benevolent being, protecting the mountains and the animals that live there. In other tales, the creature is more aggressive, capable of attacking those who venture too far into its territory. Regardless of the specific portrayal, the Yeti holds a special place in Sherpa tradition, symbolizing the mystery and majesty of the Himalayan landscape.

The Buddhist monasteries of the Himalayas also feature stories of the Yeti, with some monks claiming to have encountered the creature during their travels through the mountains. In fact, one of the most famous pieces of Yeti "evidence" is a scalp kept in the Khumjung Monastery in Nepal, which is said to belong to the Abominable Snowman. While the authenticity of the scalp has been questioned, it remains a focal point for Yeti enthusiasts and tourists alike.

Western Encounters with the Yeti

Western interest in the Yeti began in the 19th century, when British explorers and mountaineers traveling through the Himalayas heard stories from the local Sherpa guides about a mysterious, ape-like creature that lived in the mountains. These stories captured the imaginations of Western adventurers, many of whom hoped to find evidence of the Yeti during their expeditions.

One of the earliest documented encounters with the Yeti occurred in 1832, when B.H. Hodgson, a British naturalist, reported seeing a "tall, bipedal creature covered in dark fur" while traveling in Nepal. Hodgson's account was dismissed by his contemporaries, who believed that he had simply seen a bear, but the story planted the seed for future Yeti sightings.

In the 1920s, the legend of the Yeti gained international attention when British mountaineers attempting to climb Mount Everest reported finding large footprints in the snow at altitudes above 20,000 feet. These footprints, which were far larger than any known animal tracks, were attributed to the Yeti, and the media quickly latched onto the story. Newspapers across the world began referring to the creature as the Abominable Snowman, a term that would become synonymous with the Yeti.

Perhaps the most famous Western encounter with the Yeti occurred during the 1951 Mount Everest expedition led by Eric Shipton, a renowned British mountaineer. While exploring the Menlung Glacier, Shipton and his team discovered a series of large, humanoid footprints in the snow. Shipton took several photographs of the prints, which measured 13 inches long and featured distinct toes and arches. These photographs became iconic in Yeti lore, sparking renewed interest in the creature and inspiring a new generation of cryptozoologists to take up the search.

Major Expeditions and Scientific Investigations

Over the years, numerous expeditions have been launched to find evidence of the Yeti, with varying degrees of success. Some of the most famous and well-funded expeditions took place in the 1950s and 1960s, when the Yeti became a focal point for cryptozoologists and adventurers alike.

1. The 1954 Daily Mail Expedition:

In 1954, the British newspaper The Daily Mail sponsored an expedition to Nepal in search of the Yeti. The expedition, led by John Angelo Jackson, focused on investigating the footprints found by Shipton in 1951. The team spent several weeks exploring the region around Mount Everest and Annapurna, interviewing local Sherpas and collecting evidence of the Yeti's existence.

While the expedition did not find the creature itself, the team did discover several more sets of unusual footprints and managed to obtain hair samples from what the Sherpas claimed was a Yeti. These hair samples were later analyzed by British scientists, who concluded that they likely came from a bear or yak, but the results were inconclusive.

2. The Tom Slick Expeditions:

In the late 1950s, American oil tycoon Tom Slick funded a series of expeditions to the Himalayas in search of the Yeti. Slick, a passionate cryptozoologist, believed that the creature could be a living relic of an ancient hominid species, such as Gigantopithecus or Homo erectus.

Slick's teams conducted extensive searches in Nepal and Tibet, collecting footprints, scat samples, and even Yeti dung, which was analyzed for DNA. While Slick's expeditions failed to find definitive proof of the Yeti, they helped to solidify the creature's place in cryptozoology and inspired future expeditions.

DNA Testing and the Yeti Debate

In recent years, advancements in DNA analysis have brought new tools to the search for the Yeti. Several hair and bone samples attributed to the Yeti have been collected over the years, and scientists have conducted genetic testing to determine their origins.

One of the most notable DNA studies on Yeti samples was conducted in 2014 by a team of researchers led by Bryan Sykes, a geneticist at Oxford University. Sykes and his team analyzed hair samples from supposed Yeti sightings and compared the DNA to known species. The results were surprising: the DNA matched that of an ancient polar bear species, suggesting that some Yeti sightings may have been misidentifications of bears living in the high altitudes of the Himalayas.

Other DNA analyses have yielded similar results, with most Yeti samples being identified as bears, yak, or human. However, some samples have produced inconclusive results, leaving the door open for the possibility that an unknown species could still be lurking in the remote regions of the Himalayas.

Theories About the Yeti's Identity

There are several competing theories about the true identity of the Yeti. While most scientists believe that the Yeti is simply a misidentified bear, cryptozoologists and some anthropologists argue that the creature could be a relic hominid or an undiscovered primate.

1. The Bear Theory:

The most widely accepted scientific explanation for Yeti sightings is that they are the result of misidentified Himalayan brown bears or Tibetan blue bears. Both species are known to inhabit the same high-altitude regions where Yeti sightings occur, and their large size, fur-covered bodies, and ability to walk on two legs make them likely candidates for the Yeti.

In addition, bear tracks left in the snow can sometimes resemble human-like footprints, especially when the bear's front and hind legs overlap, creating the illusion of a bipedal creature.

2. The Relic Hominid Theory:

Some cryptozoologists believe that the Yeti could be a surviving population of an ancient hominid, such as Gigantopithecus, a giant ape that lived in Asia during the Pleistocene epoch. Gigantopithecus is thought to have gone extinct around 100,000 years ago, but some researchers suggest that small populations could have survived in the remote mountains of the Himalayas.

Another possibility is that the Yeti is a descendant of Homo erectus, an early human species that also lived in Asia. Supporters of this theory argue that the Yeti's human-like features and ability to walk upright make it more likely to be a hominid than a bear.

Skepticism and the Challenges of Yeti Research

While the Yeti remains one of the most famous cryptids in the world, the search for definitive evidence has been fraught with challenges. The harsh environment of the Himalayas makes it difficult for researchers to conduct long-term investigations, and the remote locations where Yeti sightings occur are often inaccessible for much of the year.

Skeptics argue that the lack of physical evidence—such as bones, bodies, or nests—strongly suggests that the Yeti does not exist. They point to the overwhelming evidence that most Yeti sightings are simply cases of misidentified bears and argue that the legend persists primarily due to its cultural significance and the allure of the unknown.

However, the Yeti's place in Sherpa tradition and the numerous credible sightings by mountaineers and explorers ensure that the legend will endure, even in the absence of conclusive proof.

Conclusion: The Enduring Mystery of the Yeti

The legend of the Yeti continues to captivate the imaginations of people around the world. Whether the creature is a relic hominid, an undiscovered species of primate, or simply a bear living in the remote reaches of the Himalayas, the Yeti represents humanity's enduring fascination with the mysterious and the unknown.

For the Sherpa people, the Yeti is more than just a cryptid; it is a symbol of the power and majesty of the mountains, a guardian of nature that commands both respect and fear. For cryptozoologists, the Yeti represents one of the last great mysteries of our world, a creature that, if discovered, would challenge our understanding of evolution and the natural world.

As long as there are those willing to brave the harsh conditions of the Himalayas in search of the Abominable Snowman, the legend of the Yeti will endure.

THE GLOBAL HUNT
FOR CRYPTIDS

I ntroduction to the Worldwide Search for Cryptids
While creatures like Bigfoot and the Loch Ness Monster
dominate Western cryptid lore, cryptids are not exclusive to
North America and Europe. Across the globe, various cultures
have reported encounters with strange creatures that defy
scientific explanation. From the jungles of Sumatra to the rivers
of the Congo, cryptozoologists have sought to uncover the truth
behind these elusive creatures.

This chapter will explore some of the most famous cryptids
from around the world, such as the Orang Pendek of Sumatra,
the Mokele-Mbembe of the Congo, and the Bunyip of Australia.
We will examine the expeditions that have sought to find these
creatures, the cultural significance of each cryptid, and the
challenges researchers face when investigating sightings in some
of the most remote regions on Earth.

The Orang Pendek: Sumatra's Mystery Ape
The Orang Pendek, which translates to "short person" in
Indonesian, is a cryptid said to inhabit the rainforests of Sumatra,
an island in Indonesia known for its rich biodiversity and dense
jungle. The Orang Pendek is described as a small, bipedal ape-like
creature, standing around 3-5 feet tall. Unlike Bigfoot, the Orang

Pendek is believed to have a more human-like face, shorter hair, and may be a surviving species of an early hominid or a new type of great ape.

The indigenous Kubu people have spoken of the Orang Pendek for centuries, regarding the creature as part of the natural world. In their culture, the Orang Pendek is seen as elusive but intelligent, a creature that lives deep in the forest and avoids human contact. Western interest in the Orang Pendek began in the late 19th century when Dutch colonists in Sumatra reported seeing the creature. Over the years, numerous expeditions have been launched in an attempt to capture evidence of the Orang Pendek, though definitive proof remains elusive.

Modern Expeditions
One of the most notable expeditions in search of the Orang Pendek was conducted by British researcher Debbie Martyr in the 1990s. Martyr, a journalist-turned-cryptozoologist, spent over a decade in the jungles of Sumatra, interviewing locals and conducting field research. She reported several encounters with the Orang Pendek and collected footprints that she claimed could not be attributed to any known animal species in the region.
In addition to Martyr's work, other researchers have used camera traps and hair samples in an attempt to prove the Orang Pendek's existence. In one instance, footprints believed to belong to the Orang Pendek were found and cast, but no conclusive DNA evidence has been recovered.

Cultural Significance
In the Sumatran rainforest, the Orang Pendek occupies a place of reverence and respect. To the Kubu and other indigenous groups, the Orang Pendek is part of the natural landscape, much like other animals in the forest. This respect for the creature is rooted in their animist beliefs, where all living beings possess spiritual significance. The Kubu also view the Orang Pendek as a protector

of the forest, a symbol of the untamed wilderness.

In Western culture, the Orang Pendek has taken on a different role —one of a living fossil that could prove the survival of an ancient species. Cryptozoologists often link the Orang Pendek to the discovery of the Hobbit-like hominid species, Homo floresiensis, found on the nearby island of Flores. While no direct connection has been established, the possibility of an unknown primate living in Sumatra continues to fuel research and speculation.

Mokele-Mbembe: The Last Dinosaur of the Congo

The Mokele-Mbembe, often referred to as Africa's answer to the Loch Ness Monster, is said to inhabit the remote rivers and swamps of the Congo Basin in Central Africa. Descriptions of the creature closely resemble a sauropod dinosaur, with a long neck, large body, and tail. Some reports claim that the Mokele-Mbembe is amphibious and spends most of its time submerged in rivers, only surfacing occasionally.

The legend of the Mokele-Mbembe originates from the BaAka pygmies who live along the Congo River. In their oral history, the creature is both feared and respected, known for its ability to disrupt the river and destroy canoes. The Mokele-Mbembe is believed to feed on plants and can be highly territorial, reportedly attacking humans who come too close to its habitat.

Early Expeditions in Search of Mokele-Mbembe

The first known Western expedition in search of the Mokele-Mbembe took place in the early 20th century, when German explorer Captain Freiherr von Stein zu Lausnitz reported hearing about a large, dinosaur-like creature from the local people. His accounts piqued the interest of cryptozoologists and adventurers alike, leading to a series of expeditions throughout the 1900s and early 2000s.

One of the most famous expeditions was led by American

cryptozoologist Roy Mackal in the 1980s. Mackal, a biologist from the University of Chicago, believed that the Mokele-Mbembe could be a surviving species of dinosaur. His team traveled deep into the Congo Basin, interviewing locals and searching for physical evidence. While Mackal's expedition did not yield direct sightings of the creature, he gathered enough anecdotal evidence to convince him that the Mokele-Mbembe could be real.

Challenges in the Congo Basin
The dense jungles and swamps of the Congo Basin present significant challenges for researchers. The region is extremely remote and difficult to access, and the harsh conditions make long-term expeditions perilous. In addition to environmental factors, political instability and health risks such as malaria and disease further complicate fieldwork.

Despite these challenges, the search for Mokele-Mbembe continues. Modern expeditions often use satellite imagery, drone technology, and DNA sampling of the local water sources to try and detect signs of the creature. However, much like Nessie, no conclusive physical evidence has been found to support the existence of a large, dinosaur-like animal in the Congo.

The Bunyip: Australia's Mystery Water Beast
The Bunyip is a cryptid rooted in the folklore of Australia's indigenous Aboriginal peoples. Described as a creature that lives in rivers, swamps, and billabongs, the Bunyip is said to have sharp claws, a dog-like face, and a body covered in feathers or fur. Some accounts describe the Bunyip as an amphibious predator, capable of dragging people or livestock into the water.

For the Aboriginal people, the Bunyip is a spirit creature, often associated with danger and death. It is seen as a guardian of waterholes, and those who disturb its territory are said to risk a fatal encounter. The name "Bunyip" is believed to come from the Wemba-Wemba language, meaning "devil" or "evil spirit."

In the 19th century, European settlers in Australia began reporting encounters with mysterious creatures that resembled the Bunyip described in Aboriginal lore. These reports coincided with the discovery of large fossilized bones in riverbeds, leading some to believe that the Bunyip could be a prehistoric creature that had survived into modern times.

19th-Century Encounters and Fossil Discoveries
One of the most famous Bunyip sightings occurred in 1845 when a series of strange tracks were found along the banks of the Murrumbidgee River in New South Wales. The tracks were described as large and webbed, similar to those of a giant amphibian. The discovery led to widespread speculation, and local newspapers published stories about the possibility of a living Bunyip in the area.

Around the same time, explorers and farmers began unearthing large bones near rivers and swamps. These bones were initially thought to belong to the Bunyip, but further analysis revealed that they likely came from extinct marsupials, such as the Diprotodon, a giant wombat-like creature that lived in Australia during the Pleistocene epoch.

Modern Investigations
While Bunyip sightings have become less frequent in modern times, cryptozoologists and historians continue to study the creature's place in Australian folklore. Some researchers believe that the Bunyip legend could be based on encounters with unusual animals, such as saltwater crocodiles, which can grow to enormous sizes and are capable of living in freshwater habitats. Others argue that the Bunyip is a product of Aboriginal spirituality, representing a metaphor for the dangers of the natural world.

Today, the Bunyip remains an enduring part of Australia's cultural identity, appearing in art, literature, and popular media. The search for physical evidence continues, with some researchers exploring cave paintings and rock carvings that depict Bunyip-like creatures as potential clues to the cryptid's origins.

Cryptids in the Deep: Sea Serpents and Aquatic Monsters
Beyond the rivers and jungles, the oceans of the world hold some of the most enduring and terrifying cryptids. From the legendary Kraken to the elusive Globsters that wash up on beaches, the seas have long been believed to harbor creatures unknown to science. The sheer size and depth of the ocean mean that much of it remains unexplored, leading to endless speculation about what might lurk beneath the waves.

The Kraken: Myth or Reality?
The Kraken, a massive sea monster from Scandinavian folklore, is often depicted as a giant octopus or squid capable of dragging entire ships to the bottom of the ocean. First mentioned in Norse sagas dating back to the 13th century, the Kraken has inspired fear in sailors for centuries. Early descriptions of the Kraken claimed that the creature was so large that it was often mistaken for a small island, only to rise from the depths and attack unsuspecting ships.

While the Kraken was long thought to be a myth, modern discoveries of giant squid measuring over 40 feet in length have led some to speculate that the creature may have been based on real encounters with deep-sea cephalopods. In 2004, a giant squid was captured on film for the first time, providing tangible evidence of the existence of these elusive creatures.

Globsters and Other Ocean Mysteries
Globsters are another oceanic cryptid that has fascinated researchers. These large, amorphous masses of flesh have washed up on beaches around the world, often leading to speculation that they are the remains of unknown sea creatures. One of the most famous cases occurred in 1960, when a massive, unidentified blob

washed ashore in Tasmania. Initial reports suggested that the creature could be a sea monster or the remains of a prehistoric animal, but further analysis indicated that the globster was likely the decayed remains of a whale.

Despite the skepticism, globsters continue to appear on shores, sparking debate about the potential for undiscovered species in the depths of the ocean.

Case Study: The Hunt for Mokele-Mbembe

One of the most persistent and well-documented searches for an aquatic cryptid is the ongoing effort to find the Mokele-Mbembe in the Congo Basin. As mentioned earlier, the creature is believed by some to be a surviving dinosaur, and expeditions in search of it have been conducted for over a century.

One of the most significant recent expeditions took place in 2001, when a team led by cryptozoologist William Gibbons and conservationist Michel Ballot ventured into the Likouala Swamp. The team interviewed local villagers who claimed to have seen the creature and spent weeks searching the dense jungle for signs of its presence.

While the team did not find the Mokele-Mbembe, they did gather a wealth of information from locals who consistently described a creature with a long neck, small head, and massive body —a description eerily similar to that of a sauropod dinosaur. The expedition also uncovered strange tracks and unexplained disturbances in the water, but no conclusive evidence of the creature's existence was found.

Conclusion: The Global Fascination with Cryptids

From the rainforests of Sumatra to the rivers of the Congo, the search for cryptids is a global phenomenon that transcends borders and cultures. These mysterious creatures capture the imagination because they represent the possibility that there are still unknown species waiting to be discovered. Whether cryptids like the Orang Pendek, Mokele-Mbembe, or Bunyip are based in reality or are simply products of folklore and misidentification, they continue to inspire researchers, explorers, and everyday people alike.

The search for cryptids is not just a quest for the unknown—it's a testament to the human desire to explore the boundaries of knowledge and challenge the limits of what we believe to be possible.

THE TOOLS OF THE CRYPTOZOOLOGIST: METHODS, TECHNOLOGY, AND CHALLENGES

I ntroduction to Cryptozoological Methods
Cryptozoology may not have the same standing as mainstream scientific disciplines, but its researchers employ a wide array of techniques in their investigations. Cryptozoologists rely on a blend of traditional fieldwork, advanced technology, and even forensic science to hunt for evidence of elusive creatures like Bigfoot, the Loch Ness Monster, and the Chupacabra.

This chapter explores the tools and methods cryptozoologists use to search for cryptids, from motion-activated cameras and thermal imaging to DNA testing and eyewitness interviews. We'll also delve into the challenges cryptozoologists face in gathering reliable evidence, including the impact of hoaxes, environmental conditions, and the inherent difficulties of proving the existence of something that has never been captured.

Field Research: Tracking, Trapping, and Observation

At the heart of cryptozoological research is fieldwork. Cryptozoologists spend weeks or even months in remote locations, tracking cryptids, setting up traps, and making observations. They must be well-versed in tracking animals and understanding their behavior to identify clues that might point to the presence of a cryptid.

1. Footprint Casting:

One of the most iconic tools of the cryptozoologist is the plaster cast, used to preserve tracks found in the wild. Cryptozoologists often discover large footprints attributed to cryptids like Bigfoot or the Yeti, and making a plaster cast of the prints allows them to preserve the evidence for further study. These casts are analyzed to determine the size, depth, and anatomical features of the footprints.

2. Bait and Camera Traps:

Many cryptozoologists use bait and camera traps to try to capture cryptids on film. These traps are often placed in remote areas where sightings have occurred, and they are equipped with motion sensors that trigger the camera when something passes by. Bait, such as food or objects of interest, is used to lure the cryptid to the camera's field of view.

Interviewing Eyewitnesses: Balancing Skepticism and Belief

Cryptozoologists often begin their investigations by interviewing eyewitnesses who claim to have seen a cryptid. These interviews are crucial for gathering information about the location, appearance, and behavior of the creature, but they also present challenges. Eyewitness testimony can be unreliable, as memories may fade over time, and people may misinterpret what they have seen.

1. Investigating Consistency:

One of the key tasks in interviewing witnesses is to look for consistencies between reports. If multiple people describe the same creature with similar features, it lends credibility to the sightings. Cryptozoologists often collect witness accounts from different regions and compare them for similarities.

2. Psychological Factors:

Psychological factors, such as expectation, fear, and cultural influences, can affect what a witness believes they saw. Cryptozoologists must navigate these complexities, maintaining a healthy skepticism while remaining open to the possibility that the witness encountered something unknown.

Using Forensics: Hair, Footprints, and Biological Samples

Advances in forensic science have given cryptozoologists new tools to analyze potential evidence. Hair samples, footprints, and even blood or scat found in the field can be tested to determine their origin. However, the process of gathering and analyzing these samples is fraught with challenges.

1. Hair and DNA Testing:

Hair samples believed to belong to cryptids are often sent to laboratories for DNA analysis. While many samples turn out to belong to known animals, such as bears, dogs, or deer, some have produced inconclusive results, fueling speculation that the samples might come from an unknown species. DNA testing has been particularly prominent in the search for Bigfoot, with several high-profile studies generating excitement and controversy.

2. Footprint Depth and Gait Analysis:

When analyzing footprints, cryptozoologists pay close attention to the depth and gait of the tracks. Deep footprints may suggest a creature of significant weight, and the spacing of the prints can reveal whether the creature was walking upright. In some cases, footprints believed to belong to a cryptid have turned out to be hoaxes, created by people using wooden foot-shaped cutouts.

3. Scat and Tissue Samples:
On rare occasions, cryptozoologists may find scat or tissue samples that they believe belong to a cryptid. These samples are carefully collected and sent to laboratories for analysis, but like hair samples, they often turn out to belong to known animals. Nevertheless, the possibility of finding biological evidence keeps cryptozoologists motivated.

The Role of Technology: Drones, Sonar, and DNA Testing
Modern technology has revolutionized cryptozoology, giving researchers new tools to search for elusive creatures in ways that were previously impossible. From drones and thermal imaging to DNA testing and sonar scanning, cryptozoologists now have access to a wide array of high-tech gadgets to aid in their investigations.

1. Drone Technology:
Drones equipped with cameras and thermal sensors allow cryptozoologists to cover large areas of difficult terrain without having to physically enter dangerous or remote locations. Drones have been used in the search for Bigfoot, Thunderbirds, and other land-based cryptids, allowing researchers to scan forests and mountaintops from the sky.

2. Sonar Scanning:
In aquatic cryptid investigations, such as the search for the Loch Ness Monster, sonar scanning is a key tool. Sonar can detect objects deep underwater, revealing the presence of large, moving creatures that might otherwise remain hidden. Expeditions like Operation Deepscan used sonar to search for Nessie in the depths of Loch Ness, though no definitive evidence was found.

3. Environmental DNA (eDNA):
Environmental DNA (eDNA) testing is one of the newest tools in cryptozoology. This method involves collecting water or soil

samples and analyzing them for traces of DNA left behind by organisms. eDNA has been used to search for cryptids like Nessie, with researchers testing water samples from Loch Ness for signs of an unknown creature. While no conclusive results have been obtained so far, eDNA testing has shown promise as a method for identifying undiscovered species.

The Challenges of Proving the Unprovable
Despite the advances in technology and forensic science, cryptozoologists face an uphill battle in proving the existence of cryptids. The lack of physical evidence, the remote locations where cryptids are said to live, and the prevalence of hoaxes make the search for cryptids particularly difficult.

1. The Elusive Nature of Cryptids:
One of the biggest challenges in cryptozoology is that cryptids are, by their very nature, elusive. They are often described as highly intelligent and capable of avoiding human contact, which makes them difficult to track. This elusiveness is compounded by the remote and inaccessible areas where many cryptids are believed to live.

2. Hoaxes and Misidentifications:
Hoaxes have plagued cryptozoology for decades, with individuals fabricating evidence, such as fake footprints or doctored photos, to gain attention. These hoaxes damage the credibility of legitimate researchers and make it harder to discern real evidence from the fake. In addition, many cryptid sightings turn out to be misidentifications of known animals or natural phenomena, further complicating the search.

Case Study: The Cottingley Fairies and the Power of Hoaxing
One of the most famous hoaxes in cryptozoology and paranormal research is the Cottingley Fairies. In 1917, two young girls from Cottingley, England, took a series of photographs that appeared

to show fairies dancing in the woods. The photos captured the public's imagination, and even Sir Arthur Conan Doyle, the author of Sherlock Holmes, endorsed the photographs as genuine evidence of the existence of fairies.

For decades, the Cottingley Fairy photographs were hailed as proof of the supernatural, but in 1983, the girls admitted that the photographs were fakes, created using paper cutouts of fairies. The Cottingley Fairy hoax serves as a cautionary tale for cryptozoologists, highlighting the need for skepticism and rigorous analysis in the search for the unknown.

Conclusion: The Ongoing Quest for Evidence

Despite the challenges, the search for cryptids continues, driven by the desire to uncover the mysteries of the natural world. Cryptozoologists face significant obstacles in proving the existence of these elusive creatures, but the advancement of technology and forensic science has given researchers new tools to aid in their quest.

Ultimately, cryptozoology is not just about finding cryptids— it's about expanding the boundaries of what we know about the natural world. While many cryptids may never be proven to exist, the search for them represents the enduring human fascination with the unknown and the uncharted.

THE PSYCHOLOGY OF CRYPTID SIGHTINGS

Introduction: Why Do People See Cryptids?
Cryptid sightings are reported across the world, yet despite the prevalence of these reports, definitive evidence of cryptids remains elusive. How do we explain the thousands of people who claim to have seen Bigfoot, the Loch Ness Monster, the Mothman, or other mysterious creatures? The answer may lie in the complex relationship between psychology, perception, and belief.

This chapter explores the psychological factors that contribute to cryptid sightings, including cognitive bias, cultural influence, and the role of fear and expectation in shaping what people see. We'll examine why some people are more likely to believe in cryptids than others and delve into the concept of mass hysteria and social contagion as explanations for widespread cryptid sightings.

Cognitive Bias and Cryptid Sightings
Cognitive bias refers to the way our brains process information and make judgments based on prior experiences, expectations, and emotions. In the context of cryptid sightings, several types of cognitive bias can play a role in shaping what people believe they've seen.

1. Pareidolia: Seeing Patterns in Random Stimuli

Pareidolia is a cognitive phenomenon in which the brain perceives familiar patterns, such as faces or animals, in random stimuli. For example, people may see shapes in clouds or faces in the bark of a tree. In cryptid sightings, pareidolia can lead witnesses to interpret ambiguous visual cues, such as shadows or movement, as evidence of a cryptid.

In many Bigfoot sightings, for example, witnesses may see a dark shape in the distance and interpret it as a large, bipedal creature, when in reality it could be a bear, tree, or even a trick of the light. Pareidolia plays a significant role in sightings of cryptids like the Loch Ness Monster, where waves or floating debris in the water may be mistaken for a long, serpentine creature.

2. Confirmation Bias: Seeing What You Want to See
Confirmation bias occurs when people seek out information that confirms their preexisting beliefs while ignoring or dismissing evidence that contradicts those beliefs. In the case of cryptid sightings, confirmation bias can lead witnesses to interpret ordinary events in ways that support the existence of cryptids.

For example, a person who already believes in Bigfoot may interpret strange sounds in the forest as evidence of the creature's presence, even though those sounds could easily be explained by known animals. Confirmation bias reinforces belief in cryptids by filtering out contradictory evidence, making it difficult for people to question their own experiences.

3. Expectation and Perception
Expectation plays a powerful role in shaping perception. When people expect to see something, they are more likely to perceive it, even if it's not really there. This phenomenon is particularly relevant in cryptid hotspots, where people are primed to look for evidence of creatures like Bigfoot or Nessie.

For example, tourists visiting Loch Ness may be more likely to interpret ripples or waves in the water as the Loch Ness Monster because they are expecting to see something out of the ordinary. Similarly, people hiking in areas known for Bigfoot sightings may interpret sounds or shapes as evidence of the creature, even if there's a rational explanation.

Cultural Influence and the Role of Media
Culture and media play a significant role in shaping how people perceive and report cryptid sightings. Popular culture has elevated certain cryptids, such as Bigfoot and the Loch Ness Monster, to near-mythic status, and the imagery of these creatures is deeply ingrained in the collective imagination.

1. The Influence of Popular Culture
Television shows, films, books, and online communities dedicated to cryptids have a profound influence on public perceptions of these creatures. The Patterson-Gimlin film of 1967, which purportedly shows Bigfoot walking through a forest in Northern California, became a cultural touchstone, cementing the image of Bigfoot as a large, hairy, bipedal ape. This image has since been reinforced through countless documentaries, TV shows, and movies, shaping how people expect Bigfoot to look and behave.

When people report sightings of cryptids, their descriptions are often influenced by the popular images they've been exposed to. For instance, many people describe the Mothman as a winged, red-eyed figure, in part because that is how the creature was depicted in John Keel's book, *The Mothman Prophecies*, and the subsequent film adaptation.

2. Mass Media and Social Contagion
Mass media has the ability to spread cryptid sightings, creating a phenomenon known as social contagion. This occurs when reports of cryptid sightings spread rapidly through a community, leading more people to believe they have seen the creature. Social contagion is often fueled by news reports, television specials, and

online forums, where cryptid sightings are discussed and debated. One of the best-known examples of social contagion in cryptozoology is the Jersey Devil scare of 1909, when hundreds of people across New Jersey and Pennsylvania reported sightings of the Jersey Devil within a span of just a few days. Newspapers fueled the panic, publishing sensationalized stories of the creature attacking trolleys, flying over towns, and leaving strange tracks in the snow. The rapid spread of these reports led to mass hysteria, with people interpreting ordinary events as evidence of the Jersey Devil's presence.

Fear, Anxiety, and the Unknown

Fear and anxiety are powerful motivators in cryptid sightings. Many cryptids, such as Bigfoot, the Mothman, and the Jersey Devil, are associated with fear-inducing environments—dense forests, isolated mountains, or swampy regions—where people may feel vulnerable or threatened. In these environments, the mind may play tricks on people, leading them to perceive danger where none exists.

1. The Role of Fear in Cryptid Sightings

When people are in an environment where they feel scared or uneasy, they may be more likely to misinterpret what they see or hear. The fight-or-flight response, triggered by fear, can heighten the senses and make people more alert to potential threats. In such a state, people may interpret ordinary stimuli—such as rustling leaves or animal sounds—as evidence of a cryptid.

For example, hikers alone in a dark, dense forest may hear branches snapping and immediately associate the sound with Bigfoot, especially if they are already aware of local lore. Similarly, people walking along a fog-covered lake might interpret ripples in the water as the Loch Ness Monster.

2. Anxiety and Expectation

Anxiety can amplify the expectation to see a cryptid, particularly in areas known for such sightings. If someone is already anxious or fearful in an unfamiliar environment, their perception may become distorted, making them more likely to believe they have encountered something extraordinary.

This phenomenon is not limited to cryptid sightings—ghost sightings and encounters with the supernatural often occur in similarly anxiety-inducing environments, such as abandoned buildings or graveyards, where fear plays a significant role in shaping perception.

Case Study: The Mothman and Mass Hysteria

The Mothman sightings in Point Pleasant, West Virginia, from 1966 to 1967 provide a compelling example of how fear, anxiety, and media influence can contribute to cryptid sightings. The Mothman is described as a winged humanoid with glowing red eyes, and its appearance is often associated with impending disaster.

The first Mothman sighting occurred in November 1966, when two couples driving near the TNT Area, an abandoned munitions factory, reported seeing a large, winged creature with glowing red eyes. The sighting was quickly followed by numerous other reports, with locals claiming to have seen the creature flying over their cars or lurking near buildings.

As more sightings were reported, the media picked up the story, and the legend of the Mothman grew. Fear and anxiety spread through the community, particularly after the Silver Bridge collapsed in December 1967, killing 46 people. Many locals believed that the Mothman sightings were an omen of the disaster, and the creature became associated with tragedy and doom.

The Mothman case illustrates how mass hysteria, fueled by fear and media coverage, can lead to widespread belief in a cryptid. While some cryptozoologists continue to investigate the Mothman sightings, skeptics argue that the creature is a product of psychological suggestion, with people seeing what they expected to see based on media reports and local lore.

Skepticism and the Role of Critical Thinking

While cryptid sightings are often exciting and compelling, it's important to approach them with critical thinking and skepticism. Many sightings can be explained by natural phenomena, psychological factors, or hoaxes, and it's crucial to question the validity of evidence before accepting it as proof of a cryptid's existence.

1. The Importance of Objective Investigation

Cryptozoologists must balance their desire to believe in cryptids with the need for rigorous investigation. Objective investigation involves gathering evidence, analyzing it carefully, and considering alternative explanations. This approach helps prevent bias from clouding judgment and ensures that sightings are evaluated on their merits.

2. The Need for Skepticism in Cryptozoology

Skepticism is not about dismissing cryptid sightings outright —it's about asking the right questions and demanding credible evidence. In cryptozoology, where physical evidence is often scarce, skepticism helps maintain the **integrity** of the field by preventing unverified claims from gaining too much traction.

Conclusion: The Psychology of Belief in Cryptids

The belief in cryptids is shaped by a complex interplay of psychology, culture, fear, and expectation. While many cryptid sightings can be explained by natural phenomena or cognitive biases, the power of belief continues to drive people's fascination with these mysterious creatures. Understanding the psychological factors that influence cryptid sightings can provide valuable insights into why people see what they see and why the search for the unknown endures.

THE FUTURE OF CRYPTOZOOLOGY

Introduction: Cryptozoology in the 21st Century
As we move further into the 21st century, cryptozoology continues to evolve, shaped by advancements in technology, new discoveries in biology, and the ongoing fascination with the unknown. While many cryptids remain elusive, the search for them represents humanity's enduring desire to explore the unexplained and push the boundaries of scientific knowledge.

This final chapter will explore the future of cryptozoology, examining how emerging technologies, scientific discoveries, and shifting cultural attitudes may impact the field. We will also reflect on the role cryptids play in modern society, both as symbols of mystery and as reflections of our deepest fears and desires.

The Role of Emerging Technology in Cryptozoology
The future of cryptozoology will be shaped by emerging technologies that allow researchers to explore remote areas, gather data more efficiently, and analyze evidence with greater precision.

1. Drones and Remote Sensing Technology
Drones equipped with cameras and thermal imaging sensors

are becoming increasingly important in cryptozoological investigations. These devices allow researchers to cover vast areas of difficult terrain without having to physically enter remote or dangerous locations. Drones are particularly useful in the search for land-based cryptids like Bigfoot and Thunderbirds, as they can scan dense forests and mountainous regions from above.

In addition to drones, remote sensing technology, such as LIDAR (Light Detection and Ranging), is being used to map landscapes and identify potential hiding places for cryptids. LIDAR can penetrate dense forest canopies and reveal structures or features that are otherwise hidden from view, providing valuable data for cryptozoologists.

2. Environmental DNA (eDNA) Testing
Environmental DNA (eDNA) testing is one of the most promising new tools in cryptozoology. This technique involves collecting water, soil, or air samples from an environment and analyzing them for traces of DNA left behind by animals. eDNA has been used successfully in conservation biology to identify rare or endangered species, and it holds great potential for cryptozoology.

In the search for aquatic cryptids like the Loch Ness Monster, researchers can use eDNA to test water samples for signs of unknown species. While no definitive evidence of Nessie has been found using eDNA, the technique represents a new frontier in the search for cryptids.

Scientific Discoveries and Their Impact on Cryptozoology
Recent discoveries in paleontology and biology have reignited interest in cryptozoology by challenging our understanding of the natural world and suggesting that unknown species could still be discovered.

1. The Discovery of Homo Floresiensis

In 2003, scientists discovered the remains of Homo floresiensis, a small hominid species that lived on the Indonesian island of Flores around 50,000 years ago. The discovery of this "hobbit" species shocked the scientific community and raised the possibility that other unknown hominid species could still exist in remote areas.

Cryptozoologists have drawn parallels between Homo floresiensis and cryptids like the Orang Pendek of Sumatra, suggesting that the Orang Pendek could be a surviving population of an ancient hominid species. The discovery of Homo floresiensis has given new legitimacy to the search for relic hominids, spurring cryptozoologists to continue their investigations in Southeast Asia and other regions.

2. The Coelacanth: A Living Fossil

The discovery of the Coelacanth, a prehistoric fish thought to have gone extinct millions of years ago, is often cited by cryptozoologists as proof that living fossils can exist. In 1938, a Coelacanth was caught off the coast of South Africa, sparking worldwide interest in the idea that other "extinct" species could still be alive.

The Coelacanth's discovery serves as a reminder that the natural world still holds surprises, and cryptozoologists point to this case as evidence that cryptids like the Mokele-Mbembe or Thunderbirds could one day be found.

Cultural Shifts and the Changing Role of Cryptids

As society becomes more technologically advanced and interconnected, the role of cryptids in popular culture is also changing. Cryptids, once feared and revered as symbols of the unknown, have become icons of mystery, adventure, and environmentalism.

1. Cryptids as Environmental Symbols

In recent years, cryptids have been embraced as symbols of environmental conservation and the protection of wilderness areas. Bigfoot, for example, has become a mascot for conservation efforts in the Pacific Northwest, where the dense forests are seen as one of the last bastions of untouched wilderness.

Cryptids like the Loch Ness Monster and Orang Pendek have also become associated with the need to protect fragile ecosystems. In some cases, the search for cryptids has led to increased attention on preserving habitats that are home to endangered species, even if the cryptids themselves remain elusive.

2. The Internet and Cryptid Communities
The rise of the internet has transformed cryptozoology, allowing enthusiasts to connect with one another, share sightings, and organize expeditions. Online forums, YouTube channels, and social media groups dedicated to cryptozoology have created a global community of cryptid hunters who share a passion for the unknown.
This new era of digital communication has also democratized cryptozoology, allowing amateur researchers to contribute to the field. While this has led to an explosion of interest in cryptids, it has also made it easier for hoaxes and misinformation to spread.

The Challenges Ahead: Proving the Existence of Cryptids
Despite the advancements in technology and the growing interest in cryptozoology, proving the existence of cryptids remains an enormous challenge. The lack of physical evidence, the remote and inaccessible locations where cryptids are said to live, and the prevalence of hoaxes all make it difficult to gather credible proof.

1. The Elusive Nature of Cryptids
One of the primary obstacles to proving the existence of cryptids is their elusiveness. Cryptids like Bigfoot and the Yeti are often described as highly intelligent and capable of avoiding human detection. This makes them difficult to track, especially in vast wilderness areas where they are said to live.

Cryptozoologists must contend with the fact that many cryptids are reported in remote, inhospitable environments, such as the dense jungles of Sumatra or the frozen peaks of the Himalayas. These locations make long-term expeditions costly and dangerous, limiting the amount of research that can be conducted.

2. Hoaxes and the Need for Skepticism
Hoaxes remain a significant problem in cryptozoology, with individuals fabricating evidence in an attempt to gain attention or notoriety. These hoaxes not only damage the credibility of the field but also make it more difficult for legitimate researchers to be taken seriously.

Skepticism is crucial in cryptozoology, as researchers must carefully evaluate the evidence they gather and remain open to the possibility that sightings may have alternative explanations. While the desire to believe in cryptids is strong, critical thinking and objective investigation are essential for maintaining the integrity of the field.

The Role of Cryptids in Modern Society
Cryptids occupy a unique place in modern society, serving as symbols of mystery, adventure, and the human fascination with the unknown. While many cryptids may never be proven to exist, their enduring presence in popular culture speaks to a deeper human desire to explore the uncharted and challenge the boundaries of scientific knowledge.

Cryptids like Bigfoot, the Loch Ness Monster, and the Mothman have become cultural icons, appearing in everything from movies and TV shows to advertising and merchandise. These creatures, once feared and revered, have been transformed into symbols of curiosity and wonder.

CONCLUSION: THE ENDURING QUEST FOR THE UNKNOWN

As we look to the future of cryptozoology, one thing remains clear: the quest for the unknown will continue to captivate the human imagination. Whether cryptids are ever proven to exist or remain creatures of folklore and myth, their enduring presence in our culture speaks to our innate desire to explore the world's mysteries.

Cryptozoology may never provide all the answers, but it will always remind us that there are still undiscovered wonders in the world. As long as there are those willing to search the depths of the oceans, the heights of the mountains, and the darkest corners of the forest, the legend of cryptids will endure.

The adventure is far from over, and the world's cryptids still wait to be discovered.

DISCLAIMER

This book, Cryptid Detectives: Case Studies in Modern Cryptozoology Investigations, was written with the assistance of AI technology. The content within is based on a combination of publicly available information, speculative research, and the imaginative exploration of cryptozoology. While every effort has been made to present accurate descriptions and historical references, much of the subject matter involves folklore, eyewitness accounts, and unverified claims. Cryptids, by their very nature, are subjects of ongoing debate and investigation, and no definitive scientific proof of their existence has been confirmed.

The information provided should be interpreted as part of the broader study of cryptozoology, which often blends fact with legend, and should not be considered conclusive evidence of the existence of any specific creatures. Readers are encouraged to approach cryptozoology with an open mind, a healthy dose of skepticism, and a sense of curiosity.

This book is intended for educational and entertainment purposes and is not meant to serve as scientific documentation. The use of AI in the creation of this work is to enhance the writing process and compile research but does not substitute for the work of cryptozoologists, scientists, or researchers dedicated to the field.

Printed in Great Britain
by Amazon

54523171R00056